ZIMBABWE THE WAY FORWARD

LESSONS FROM A 20-YEAR-OLD

CRAIG L. TAPENI

Disclaimer

Although the author and publisher have made every effort to ensure that the information in this book was correct at press time, the author and publisher do not assume and hereby disclaim any liability to any party for any loss, damage, or disruption caused by errors or omissions, whether such errors or omissions result from negligence, accident, or any other cause.

ISBN 978-1-7348451-3-6 for (Paperback)

ISBN 978-1-7348451-5-0 for (E-Book)

For the young and not so old.......

"This book is highly inspirational, powerful, candid, clear and straight to the point. It's like a call to action, a call to arms, inviting us to an African dream speaking on one destination, helping us to realize that realities do not last forever, and new ones can be created. It invites us to think with our hearts not and only our heads, and above all to look at Africa as a sight of innovation and economic miracles".

George Kudzai Zharare- CEO and Founder Motapa Group

CONTENTS

Foreword

Craig has written a book that is unbelievable for his age. The concepts he introduces at the planning table in Zimbabwe are something that will be news to many much older professionals who are involved in driving Zimbabwe into the future. The book is written in very brief sections about the message he wants to put across but he does it in such a way that anyone can understand the transformational science of change, you would think that the book was written by someone with a master's degree. If it were possible for the leaders to follow his format, I have no doubt that Zimbabwe would be on the sure road to transformation in a fairly short period of time.

Craig is a very unusual young man. His quest for knowledge is very hard to beat. I got the privilege to meet him in 2018 when I went to Africa on a Pan African mission. On my way to Zambia I visited Mr Mutumwa Mawere at his office in South Africa. I was invited to participate in a discussion about African Transformation. On this show was an eighteen-year-old young man who was speaking from Zimbabwe. I was very surprised by his level of maturity and knowledge about the need for

African transformation. I was given his number because I was interested in meeting him. We arranged and met. I was very surprised even further, when he explained to me that by the age of fourteen, he was already aware about the African economic condition and how it affected us as Africans.

He was very interested in us to begin collaborating to see if he could find a way to further his interest in Pan African modernization. I happened to have done a 5-year study of the African continent, its issues and what could be done to fix them. We found common ground. I discovered his depth of history, and the people he quoted was very unusual for his age. I offered to mentor him on what to do in order to participate in Africa. I encouraged him to view himself as someone who knew most of what someone needed to know to do something about the Pan African economic revolution. I suggested that he needed to focus on what could be done to start on the journey towards a better economy and better standards of life for Africans.

I offered to tutor him and share information and teach him the science of national transformation. I had asked him what his real passion was and what he believed was the purpose he wanted to pursue. He told me that Pan African freedom was his passion. I then advised him that if he were to skip one year of college, I would hold classes with him online to study the science of change majoring in strategic transformation science. His mother was a bit worried, but I had a discussion with her, we agreed on the advantages of getting to understand more about his mission before going to college so that he wouldn't get distracted and bored because most of the students of his age were not at his level of consciousness and mostly not sure what their missions in life would be. It was critical for him to follow his passion rather than anything else as he would eventually find himself disappointed in every other commitment.

Craig became my first student at the Transformational Institute of Human Emergence that I am putting together and introducing to Africa. We had classes daily for about two years. He had been interested in writing a book. After the training he told me that he wanted to write a book about the Zimbabwean situation, I encouraged him to use that knowledge he had learned to come up with some ideas about change in Zimbabwe. He came up with the title, **"Zimbabwe the way forward,"** and here we are today.

I am convinced that this book written by a 20-year-old will open the eyes of many adults, professionals and leaders in Zimbabwe. As my first student at the Transformational Institute of Human Emergence I am very proud of Craig's performance.

Hannington Mubaiwa President of STRAVENA, founder of the Transformational Institute of Human Emergence and author of The Riot Act: An African Master Reset.

INTRODUCTION

When I went on a quest for what is wrong with Zimbabwe and Africa, I became obsessed like George Malory the British explorer who died on Mount Everest trying to climb it simply because *"it is there"*. The uplifting of the African people has always been part of my DNA, I believe even before I was born. My expected date of delivery was supposed to be the 25th of May (Africa Day) but I ended being born three days later on the 28th of the May 1999 in the month of Africa. I will tell you not a day passes without me conversing about what needs to be done in Africa and Zimbabwe whether it's with a stranger, a family member, friend or even a girlfriend if a had one.

I was blessed enough to know my mission at a very young age that many things did not matter because like Dr. Martin Luther King, *"I have been to the mountaintop"*. God has shown me the end game and I am not moving in the present anymore but into the future. I am not a prophet, but I know God talks to me through people, things and many other mediums. I am not insane nor schizophrenic, I am just a believer who is open and teachable. Some might want to call it a coincidence but to me it is Divine serendipity because you can't have the same coincidences all the time I have come to believe. It is because the things that I usually come across usually have to do with Africa or Zimbabwe can one explain that? No, ordinarily, you can't; it is the invisible hand of God that guides me.

I know you are now wondering why I am talking about divine serendipity; well it is because the story of this book is about serendipity and let me dive into it. One day, I woke up and wrote a vision board for my life and amongst the things that I was going to do was writing a book about *"What needs to be Done in Zimbabwe"*. By the way I was still eighteen so what was I going to write in that book? You see that was God talking to me and I did not know how but I just carried on with my obsession having conversations about Zimbabwe's transformation. Then one day I woke up and said to my uncle I want to have an intellectual conversation then he said, *"why don't you call 1873fm"*. 1873FM had a new show called the Nerd Galaxy that was hosted by Ian P Venganai, who happens to be my good friend, but I had been a bit reluctant to call it I don't know why. That day somehow, I just had the courage to call in and bang, there was a discussion about African transformation. Then on the other side of the line was a man who appeared to be mesmerized by what I was saying, and I was mesmerized by what he said too, and that man is Mr. Hannington Mubaiwa.

It was not the end, but instead the beginning of a new era in our lives. That is when our relationship as mentor and mentee, father and son began. Have you ever felt as if you have found something you were in pursuit of your entire life? Well… that was the mutual feeling between the both of us, I decided to understudy him and become his mentee, because I identified tons of knowledge in what he knew about National Transformation. Like any other teenager, I was going through a mid-life crisis. I knew that my path was in African Transformation, but because of family pressure, I was about to lose my mission, and go to law school. What startled me was that all my life I had never pictured my life in the court of law, but instead writing a new script of the African Transformation story. Therefore, I knew I needed consultation from the older and wiser then, Mr. Mubaiwa said me without any emotion of doubt " Craig, so school can wait, but the world will never wait for those who wait, so it's either you choose to go to school and wait for things to happen, or to pursue your God given mission and make things happen." He told me that I already had a bachelor's degree equivalent in Political Science that everyone who has a passion to change Africa has enough history and politics. What seems to be missing with many is "knowing what to do and grasping the science to make it happen. My desire to know more about this so much intriguing science behind national transformation was set on an unquenchable fire. He specifically informed me right from the beginning that we would focus more on national visionary transformative science of change. I remember him saying. "Craig, I want to turn you into a 'Whatman, 'because 'Howman' are a dime a dozen" I recall.

So, I made one of the hardest decisions in my life then, I chose not to go to Law school and commenced learning National Transformation. Every day we had four- hour conversations on WhatsApp which happened to be lectures for the next two years. As I went deeper into these studies, I began to realize that, in Zimbabwe and Africa we have plenty of people who know what to do to change Zimbabwe or Africa but somehow the system does not tap into that resource. I developed a deep desire to highlight this indispensable God given resource of Zimbabwean talent and the treasure of the knowledge content amongst our people. What I learnt from one person that sounded so powerful made me wonder what could be done to tap into this deep well of redundant African potential starting in Zimbabwe. I felt compelled to share my discovery with all the youth and the leaders of Zimbabwe. I found Mr. Mubaiwa's unwavering confidence in the science of change as our answer very unique motivational encouragement. This is where the inspiration and background knowledge to write this book came from.

This book is written from a visionary point of view, more of what it can be, and not what it is! Would you agree that many Zimbabweans know how to do things, but not what to do at the right moment? Yes… of course you do agree, well, it is because visionaries are excluded at the table of National Planning, whilst technocrats are given a golden key, on the basis of their credentials and LinkedIn profiles. I hold nothing against technocrats, but transformation should begin at a visionary space before engaging the technical aspect of it. The process of National Transformation is like building a house. You need an architect to design a plan of the future picture, which happens to be the end result. After engaging an architect, you'll need contractors to build that house, and turn that design on the plan into reality. Now in Zimbabwe, it is vice versa, we start by calling contractors, without having a plan of what we need to build! What would they produce? If we are lucky maybe, walls, but not a state-of-the-art building. **All the time, resources, and talent** wasted to produce nothing! Don't you think it's a lost cause? How do we expect to build a state-of-the-art economy, in the 21st century, when we don't follow the correct sequence?

As a broadcaster, I have been to many seminars and forums, trying to map a way forward for Zimbabwe, but we usually find ourselves back to our default state, leaving everything to the professionals. The reason why these gatherings produce little tangible, is because of what my professor calls "the dictatorship of the technocrat," where technocrats dominate in these forums, and fight for credibility amongst themselves, forgetting the main thing which is, National Building. I have tried approaching some of the reputable technocrats in Zimbabwe, but they quickly turned me away mainly because of my age, "education" credentials, without even looking at what I had to present. In the mind of an average high-profile Zimbabwean, a normal man without a P.H.D. can never ever talk or think about what could be done in Zimbabwe. They are expecting, a superficial human being, coming from Mars with five P.H.D 's, who has run multi-billion corporations, to come with an answer. Well... sweet dreams that will happen in the next life (if we happen to have one).

What many people have failed to learn from history is that, answers come from common men, not the ones running the system, because they are already contained in the system, and they see things as they are, and not what they can be! Have you ever wondered why the aero plane was invented by two men who repaired bicycles? Weren't there ship owners who traveled across seas and oceans every day? Well they never conceptualized that one day, people would want to travel across the seas and oceans faster. Maybe they did so, but they tried to make ships faster for they were convinced that, the ship was the only mode of transport to travel across the seas. Instead the Wright brothers said, "we going to fly in the sky like a bird!" and from that concept, the human race was changed forever by common men with no college education. So, my question is "does one need school to see the future?".

Why do you think, the railway kings, who controlled America, ended up being broke? It is because, they had been in business for a very long time, and they were convinced that the railway was the end, and no other transport means was going to replace it. They never thought Henry Ford and the Wright brothers were going to revolutionize cross country and continental travel. What contributed to the rise of companies like Apple and Microsoft? It was because of the short sightedness of companies like IBM and Xerox. Firstly, IBM was in the business machines and mainframe business computers; they did not conceptualize that one day every household would need a computer and held on to that idea till it was too late. The ideas which transformed the PC like the Graphic User Interface and the mouse were conceptualized at the Palo Alto Research Centre that was built by Xerox, a company that specialized in printers as a place to gather new ideas in the information era. So, it was the computer geeks who hung around PARC, who came up with the idea of the Xerox Alto that had all those components. When they presented it to their managers, they turned the idea down claiming that they were in the printing business, so they had no interest in going into the PC business. Then they were two young men, who exploited the opportunity and took the talent from PARC and created the biggest companies in the world and these two are Bill Gates and Steve Jobs who were college dropouts with no business experience but ended up winning because they saw the future.

Yahoo lost the search engine race to GOOGLE simply because they undermined an idea of page search that Larry Page and Sergey Brin presented to them in return for one million dollars (that was in 1997). It did the same mistake again in 2003 of not buying GOOGLE for the five billion dollars that they requested and undervalued it, insisting to pay three billion dollars, which let the opportunity slide. GOOGLE grew to be over half a trillion dollars in value and the biggest search engine in the world. Where is Yahoo? No one really talks about it as in the 90'sbecause of the arrogance of *bosses who don't listen to people and see things as they are not what they could be.* So why can't our leaders learn from history and listen to those who come with constructive ideas. All I am saying is that the Zimbabwean solution will not come from superficial human beings but great dreamers and a few with a gift of intuitive foresight amongst the common people of Zimbabwe.

There is a need for a clarified national vision that is charming enough to attract the needed resources and motivate the people of Zimbabwe into materializing that vision as mentioned in this book, of transforming Zimbabwe into a higher economic state with a nominal GDP of USD 1 trillion in the next 40 years, a figure that sounds crazy at first but that I totally believe in after a very simple analysis and a bit of basic Math that my mentor taught me. Mr. Mubaiwa came up with the figure of a trillion-dollar vision, because in the end it is the GDP figures which professionals look at to determine the size of an economy. From that vision, we need a leading idea which could be "making Zimbabwe the leading economy and prototype for African socio-economic Transformation."

If there is one thing that has derailed our nation of its creative capacity, *it's toxic politics!* Our nation is divided on two fronts:

1. The right
2. The left

Tensions are high on both sides, as if we are in war! *yes, we are in war, but a bloodless one.* This time it's a cold war, that has shifted its geo-political location from the East vs West (USA vs The Soviet Union) to the right vs left in Zimbabwe. I don't know who exactly coined this phrase that we have *party-riots and no patriots* in Zimbabwe, but it's relevant in the modern-day context of Zimbabwe. We have more people who owe allegiance to their party and not the nation, they applaud national issues on the basis of the party that implements it.

When Vince Lombardi took over the Green Bay Packers, he was asked if he was going to change the players, and he said that he "was going back to the brilliance of basics, "which means he was going to change the game plan and not the game players. Same as us, we cannot wipe out (or change) the entire generation of Zimbabweans, but we can change the processes that have kept us on a functional stasis for decades by what scientists love to call a paradigm shift. There is need for a new revolutionary thinking aided by a sense of urgency that something is wrong, and someone has to stand up and do something.

The harsh, but real truth, is that, we are heirs to both the successes and failures of our country. Yes, we have inherited Zimbabwe in shambles on its worst and it is up to us to choose the state in which we leave it in for the upcoming generations, but the question is *what legacy are we going to leave them?* With the rate in which we are moving, I think the only thing we can leave them is party regalia, because we have more political parties to functional industries. Our leaders seem to be focusing more on the next general election than the next generation, their vision is having political office and after that *dololo*. We have moved from being political-economic states to economic-socio-political states, so the main thing is not politics but the economy and uplifting people to a higher state. It is now time to have an economic identity on the global arena and move from preaching empty political ideologies that amount to nothing.

When all is said and done what matters isn't what we know or understand but what we implement. Let us think like men of action and act like men of thought, as Kwame Nkrumah often said. It is time to do and not to talk or decide, this is the right time to start for there is no perfect timing and no perfect person to help us bring the change. If not us then, who? If not now then, when? So, the answer is we are the answer and the time is now. This book is not "the how to" guide but instead for what I believe is to be done, it is written by a "what" man and not a how man. It focuses more on the visionary "what to be done." The how part will answer itself when we have answered the what because we have a lot of technocrats who know how to do things and they just need to be given the what, then the magic happens. A proper visionary process that creates a clear adequate vision has been a major factor that has kept us where we are. When the right vision is there, that is very clear, it has the power to make things happen regardless of all surrounding issues, because it motivates the masses to action.

This book is there to prove that we have Zimbabweans out there with answers to our problems and I will reference to concepts and examples of Zimbabwean people with a deeper understanding of the strategic science behind transforming the economy. I am just a believer who has total confidence in the undying potential of our people and it is my wish that those with creative ideas, will one day sit at the planning table regardless of their social standing.

CHAPTER ONE - ASKING THE RIGHT QUESTIONS

If you have been in Zimbabwe for quite a long time, I think you quite familiar with this question "What came first the chicken or the egg? Some say the egg; some say the chicken. Truth be told we cannot go back to trace whether it was two eggs that hatched into male and female nor whether they were just female and male chickens that mated and produced eggs.

Neither have we agreed on that nor have we achieved anything in that debate. It just drains our energy. I have given an example of the chicken and egg question, for it is similar to our change question in Zimbabwe. Go to any seminar, forum or dialogue where people are trying to map a way forward the atmosphere is always the same. Nothing comes out of it because it is like a high school debate where *"technocrats"* fight for credibility without bringing about a solution.

Philosophical fool's paradise

The two questions that stand at this moment in our nation are why isn't change coming and who will bring it?

I have come across a lot of people in Zimbabwe who are fully convinced that change won't come to Zimbabwe and they will show you a tonnage of facts and books that nothing good comes out of Zimbabwe.

I have also come across people who say we have prayed and fasted for our nation, then why isn't God answering us? There are also those who say that the *"international community"* will one day save us. All I know is that all of us here yearn for a better and prosperous Zimbabwe despite our different ideologies and beliefs.

Change is an organic and scientific process, and it needs us to approach it from the creative inside of us and not only the technical way. The problem seems to be that we are not following the science and sequence of change. We are starting with the least important question which is "How".

It's like asking yourself about the journey whether you will use a car, train or airplane without having a desired destination where would you go? The next thing that you end up doing is canceling that journey, staying where you are and never reaching anywhere.

Once you understand where you want to go, why and when you intend to be there, that is when you decide how. If you want to go to Johannesburg from Harare for a business meeting happening in the next four hours, when choosing your options; it's obvious you need the fastest means of transport and here it's the airplane!

The other question is who will bring that change we desire, and the answer is; it is the least important question it's like asking yourself who will drive me from Harare to Bulawayo? Are they qualified? I mean, all this doesn't matter if you want to go to Bulawayo you just go to the station and board a bus that is departing. It is the same as the change question who will lead it doesn't matter but what matters is, are they leading us to our desired destination.

If we continue asking ourselves the least important questions about how we are going to change Zimbabwe and who will lead the change. If we don't get the answers as soon as possible, we quickly get discouraged and drained that change is hard.

We are convinced that it can't be done, and we create what my dad calls a *Philosophical Fool's Paradise*. This a state of the psychology by which one lives with the thinking and conviction that things are impossible. These are the people who have a narrow worldview and believe that everything tough and all problems presented in front of them is a natural order of society which can never be changed.

The What Question

"Your job is not to know the how it's to know the what and be open to discovering and receiving the how" *(Anonymous)*

The first step in the process is asking ourselves WHAT needs to be done. In the science of change, **What** is the equivalent of the desired destination where one intends to be. It is like an end product which we need to see in the long run starting with the "what" is like starting with the end in mind.

Therefore, we need to start by addressing what needs to be done in Zimbabwe before anything else. The golden rule of change is that you lay down your vision before anything else.

For us to answer this question, we do not need foreign nations nor the technical expertise to do so. We just need to dream of what it is we want to be.

Let me equate nation-building to building your own house. We cannot build a state-of-the-art house without first engaging an architect to design the result on paper. We can hire the best high-level contractors but without first engaging the architectural process. They will never produce anything great despite their technical expertise, for they will be no future picture of what to produce in reality.

Like what President Roosevelt said in his 1933 inaugural address that *"Without a vision, the people will perish"*. It shows us that without addressing the *What* part we are a bus without a destination, we become an all-show no-go ride. We just move without having any progress.

The "what" question is the rarely answered question by many people and ignoring it has made the change a complicated process in the eyes of many. Let us start by addressing the *"what"*, the rest will follow, and the process shall take care of itself.

The Why and When Questions

In everything we want to do, we should be able to answer these two interrelated questions which are when and why? It is because we need to justify our vision and give it a sense of schedule.

This paves way for one to choose which means to use to get where they desire to be. It's time we decided the purpose of our vision why are we doing it and whom we are doing it for. Is it for us, those in power or the future generations?

We have to decide the time in which we want to get where we want to be. Therefore, by knowing the purpose of our vision and when we want to achieve it, we automatically answer the how part which is our strategy towards achieving our goal.

The How Question

This is the part where we select our means towards achieving our vision after we answer the what, why and when. When the why and when are strong enough the how answers itself. Many people think that it is the most important, but I say it is the least important to worry about.

It is just that we are technical in our approach when it comes to change, and it becomes a hard puzzle with many missing pieces. By first addressing the What, Why, and When automatically we answer the How part.

The Who Question

This is another impediment to Zimbabwean change because we have put much of our energy on who will lead the change without addressing the major questions. The other delusion is that we think that the person who will lead our change must be perfect and some high-level technocrat in all fields.

We are expecting a person with five PHDs, who has run many multibillion corporations, with the kind-heartedness of Mother Theresa who will come out of the sky flying to tell us that now is the time like Angel Gabriel. We think that the International community will one day wake up and endorse someone, then real change will come. No messiah will come and save our country from the misery it is today. We are our messiahs. We have prayed and fasted for our nation and God already answered us.

Many people have answers to our problems, but we doubt and ignore them. I will give you the example of the airplane; it's inventors the Wright Brothers were common men who repaired bicycles, but they changed the world. Bill Gates was a teenager at Harvard Law School who revolutionized the computer industry, but many experts and high-level people were there.

No one already swallowed up by the system will usually bring ideas that will shake the status quo. The government will never give you orders to be innovative; the majority of innovations never came from the direct orders of the government, be it Apple, Coca-Cola, Ford, Amazon nor even Nyaradzo or Econet.

None of these came from the governments' orders but from foresighted individuals and all these companies have contributed immensely to the Global and local economies. The answer is the one who sees the future first should lead us into the promised land; It can either be you or me.

If answers to the problems that we all face came from perfect individuals, then we wouldn't be having any answers because no one is perfect on this earth. We are all part of the solution and we are the ones we seek.

We have to start by asking the right questions for us to get the right answers. It is not hard to ask the right questions, but we make it hard for ourselves by leaving some elements of the questions and not following the sequence of the questions. Change is a complex but simple process.

We are just overworking our brain by overthinking and approaching our problems with an academic and technical approach other than from a divine organic social intent approach. You can never reach a new destination by using the same way you used to get to your previous destination.

Albert Einstein is believed to have said that; *"Insanity is doing the same thing over and over again and expecting different results."* It is high time we engage a new approach which is more organic to technical for us to get new results.

We might argue and argue but for Zimbabwe to get out this darkness it is in today we need a new way of thinking, doing and even asking. It is not merely about changing the driver for us to get to our destination but having a destination in the first place. Hence, it's all about us going back to the drawing board and look for a destination together.

Yes, we can change our driver if we want to but first there has to be a destination of where to go because the whole thing is not centered on the driver but the destination. In short let us have a desired destination as a people, know when and why we want to get there, choose how we get there and the one who will get us there will emerge amongst us.

CHAPTER TWO - ZIMBABWE AND THE WORLD

We are a young nation that has been there for about four decades. We have had our ups and downs like any other nation in this world. From the 1980s our lives have deteriorated; we have moved from the so-called *"Bread-basket"* status of Africa into a Pariah-State.

We have moved from being counted on to being counted out. Industries have closed and more closing without new ones being born! Our people are poverty-stricken with no indigenous access to capital! Our banks are insolvent!

Our social services have dilapidated, and we can go on and on pointing out what is wrong, and we can even write our encyclopedia! In brief, our country is in a catastrophic state both socially and industrially! We are in dire need of assistance in our country and our savior is us the people.

It is time we come together as a people putting our differences aside and finding our common denominator, which is fighting the Goliath that lies ahead of us. Our nation is on life -support, it is wounded, bleeding for its life and in urgent need of healing.

Like our African culture elaborates that when a family member is sick everyone sits down, and they decide on what to do to save their loved one's life. If it means taking them to the traditional healers, church or hospital they first have to agree on that and then start moving.

My dear brothers and sisters, in this case, I would like to remind you that our nation, our motherland, our only parent that has given birth to us is ailing and her children need to sit and find an urgent healing solution.

We will never heal our mother by fighting against each other in the name of the so-called I know what is right. A lawyer mentality in our politics of *"I am Right I can defend it"* won't heal this nation, but in fact, it will tear it apart.

No one from next door will come and nurse our sick mother without a benefit and with as much love as us. If we can't love what is ours, who will do the duty for us? The Titanic is sinking, and we are in dire need of a plan for what to do!

A House Divided Within Itself

We are on one bus, the people in it want to go to different places all at once and they all want to get there, but they do not know exactly where. The problem is that everyone thinks where they want to go to is the best place to be for that is the only place they know.

These people cannot have a dialogue, share ideas about the places they know and decide on the best destination to go. Now even the drivers that try to move that bus cannot move it for they do not even know where to go for its so disorganized. Even if a new driver comes into the bus and then try to move it, they always come back to the terminus they too do not know whom to listen to.

So now the passengers always find themselves at the terminus looking for a new driver and the same problem arises. The people always blame the drivers for failing to get them to their destination. These people never ask themselves what part they could have played towards getting to their destination. They always find fault in the drivers and they always hire and fire them!

The passengers never realize that they are to blame too, for they do not have ONE destination! Too many opinions, too much pride and I know it all has killed our nation. We have to realize that nation-building is not a high school debate competition or a court proceeding wherein both instances, people argue their way out.

With such a mentality our country will never go forward. We can go on for the next decade, century, or even wait for Christ's second coming with nothing changing. We were born to be interdependent on one another and not to be independent of one another. We are like the human body when one part is not working properly or goes missing then the body becomes disabled. Going against one another or trying to confront our struggle independently we can never win the war but remain stranded in the bush.

Stranded Economy

As much as we have high-level people in Zimbabwe, experts amongst experts, all the needed vast mineral resources we are a desperate and destitute economy with nowhere to go. If an economy was a person, I would like to believe that ours would be homeless belonging nowhere.

It is not because our people are clue-less, but it is because our approach is more tactical than strategic, our approach is more transactional to transformational, technical to organic, more of logic over imagination and we have forgotten the Higher Force.

1.*STRATEGY VS TACTIC*- A strategy is an overall game plan an organization uses to achieve both its long term and short-term goal tactic is a short-term policy or decision aimed at solving a particular problem or meeting a specific part of the overall strategy

Truth be told the way in which Zimbabwe is been run is tactical over being strategic. It is mainly because of issues such as trying to get the popular vote or for political mileage. Trying to appease one another or to appease the "International community" won't rebuild our country; instead will keep us roaming around in one place and behind the world.

We should stop trying to implement policies for clout or wooing monetary institutions because the results will always be negative for our people.

Our approach should be designed to achieve our vision, which is rebuilding and transforming Zimbabwe. I believe that we won't rebuild Zimbabwe by clearing arrears in the IMF or cutting government spending on social services, using clout or by politicking our opponents to get into office.

There is an African proverb that says, *"To get lost is to know the way,"* and I believe that we have been lost for a very long time and it is high time we found our way. We need to try a new way to get to a new destination before we get stranded in the jungle because sooner or later, we will die from hunger or get eaten by the beasts.

2 *TRANSACTIONAL vs TRANSFORMATIONAL*

Below is a diagram designed by my professor Hannington Mubaiwa explaining the difference between Transactional and Transformation change.

OLD PARADIGM

NEW PARADIGM

Structural
Technical

Organic

| Sustain Process | Old Era | Process Based of Present | Strategic | New Era | Visionary Based of Future |

Transactional/Evolutionary

Transformational/ Revolutionary

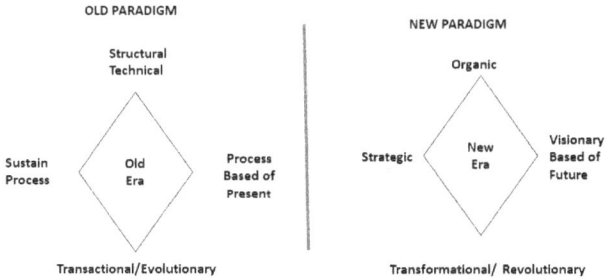

*Psychodynamics for purpose of
this book is the "new" science
of the mental creation of a new
psychology on the foundation and
the drive of inner God infused powers.*

Created by Hannington Mubaiwa

Here is another myopia that has resulted in our destitution which is that we want transformational change, but our approach is more transactional. We want to fix things one -by- one, we are focusing on inconsequential and not the main! We are looking for quick fixes and we think of replacing and repairing the *"critical parts of the engines"* forgetting that both the engine and vehicle body are dead.

The way we are doing our things is quite absurd for its like we want to install a windows 10 supported software on an MS-Dos 95 machine. When it fails, we try to change the components of the computer then the machine crushes, we cry foul and again we look for the same type of machine.

I guess maybe we are too busy to realize that we are wasting resources and time all we just have to do is to buy a new machine that works with our software without hustle.

We have been using the same way ever since this nation was born and now, we are failing to see that times are changing. We either arrested by the old thinking and paradigms as if we have a perpetual contract with them. We are in a dilapidated house, but we are painting it to look new instead of building another one.

We are scared to let go of certain things and those same things that we are afraid to let go of are the same ones impeding us from progressing. We are like that so-called born-again murderer who wants to be righteous but at the same time, he only needs to kill a few people.

3. *TECHNICAL vs ORGANIC*

If there is a word that has lost its meaning and slowly becoming cliché is none other than the word technocrat. I hold nothing against technocrats, I respect technocrats, but I think the system has made it seem as if they breathe flavored oxygen and they are superior to everyone else in our community.

Now we are stuck in the thinking that they have all the answers to our problems, and we task them with a huge burden on their shoulders. The process of change requires us to start at the organic(visionary) space, whereby we use more of our imagination before we engage logic.

As Albert Einstein states that *"Logic will get us from point A to point B, but imagination will get us everywhere"* If we don't imagine ourselves in a different place we will never get there. Same as, if we are always logical about where we are all the time we will always be stranded in that place.

Like I mentioned before that you can hire the best contractors who built the best building in the world and they can fail to produce a state-of-the-art building. Why? Simply because there is no architect in the process; hence, they will be no clear future picture of what it is that you want to produce.

That is the tragedy that has befallen our nation at this moment which is our visions are more technical to organic. Whatever we produce we do not produce from the heart and imagination we produce from academic prowess and technical expertise; hence that is why we have failed to rebuild Zimbabwe.

Just come to think of it that it all starts with imagination, even school started as an imagination. Never underestimate the power of imagination ...even weapons of mass destruction came from imagination. I believe that imagination is more powerful than reality meaning we should learn to imagine what it could be and stop trying to tackle what it is.

We also need to understand that reality is also the imagination brought to life. Realities do not last for long and new realities can also be created as I would like to say that the future has no expert, analyst, technocrat because no one has lived it! Instead, the future has an architect who designs it. Like what Abraham Lincoln says, *"the best way of predicting the future is by creating it"*.

We ought to move from the technical space into a visionary space if we want to be in a success and not stranded mode.

4.   THE HIGHER FORCE

Just because of school, we have been packaged into professionals and academics and we have lost our organic and divine space. We have been packaged with solutions in our field of expertise and we go into society looking for problems to fix in what we have been trained to be.

We forget that we were given divine power to be whatever we want to be. We do not tackle things leaving space for the Higher force to intervene, but we give our all to our technical expertise. We have never been given the space to use our organic intellectual thinking.

Because of technical expertise and how the education system was structured, we are never taught to think with our hearts but only with our heads. The education system has been designed to make us think too much and feel too little. Also, it has been structured to make our resort more to our technical expertise than our organic thinking and the *"The Higher Force."*

Therefore, I say unto you that our struggle is not just political nor socio-economic alone but also has a spiritual side of it. We have neglected the Highest Force our true Invisible Hand, which is God.

No human being can carry the weight of the world, for we only have two hands. We all need that third hand to sustain us when we get tired and weary.

I believe that our job is to know what we want, surrender it to the Higher force and He will give us the "How," and naturally, the laws of nature will take control of it.

Three Industrial Revolutions Behind

We need to realize one thing as Zimbabweans that the world is moving at a faster pace than ever before. It's a race to the top. Every nation is looking for global significance and ways to create generational wealth.

Some might want to call it a delusion. I would love to call it a different school of thought which is that we think the world cannot move without us and one day they will come and invite us

Or maybe that the world would come to Zimbabwe on bended knee with a proposal for us to engage them in developing us. Well, if that is what you think sweet dreams keep on sleeping like Sleeping Beauty until Prince Charming comes to wake you up.

No one will invite us for they are all caught up in their national affairs to which they owe their existence. Maybe it does not hurt to see what others are doing and invite ourselves to catch up with our counterparts. Slowly but surely, we are becoming out of date for what we have is no longer needed in this day and age.

The world is going towards a fourth Industrial Revolution and we as a nation haven't been to the Second Industrial Revolution. Honestly speaking, we are behind in time and we are three Industrial Revolutions behind. Our gap with the world has left us in a fragile and vulnerable state for we are open to hegemony and being obsolete.

So, whether we like it or not, our nation needs a savior faster than sooner. That savior is us who will move out of the mud and make us catch up with the rest of the world.

The World we live in today

We are a young nation with a lot to offer to this world, but the world is moving at a faster pace than ever before. Unfortunately, no one will invite us to be part of the journey for they are focused on their destinations and they can't carry our weight. We ought to invite ourselves, start our journey and catch up with the rest of the world. Henceforth, we have to understand two fundamentals which are:

1 Global Connectivity

Globalization is a sweeping force that is spreading like wildfire without giving a warning shot or even raising a red flag like what Stan Davis would love to call *The Blur Effect*.

Before you know it, the direction of the ship changes and we are already going south. The saddest thing is you cannot go towards your direction. The wind will overpower you and move you in its direction. All we ought to do is to adjust swiftly in a more positive way for us to use it as leverage to get to our destination faster.

For Global Connectivity to work in our favor we need to stop political rhetoric and chauvinism of following principles based on who is our enemy or who is our friend.

Adam Smith implies in **The Wealth of Nations** that *"It is not from the benevolence of the butcher, the brewer, or the baker, that we expect our dinner but from their regard to their interest"*. Since we have a permanent interest and a long-term vision to transform our country, we should look both east, west, south and north as markets not foes and allies.

No nation is a friend to another country, but it is just a strategic partnership for both countries to pursue their self-interests in a mutually beneficial way according to my understanding and worldview.

Global connectivity is not a scapegoat for mimicking models from other nations but instead a process to apply what is applicable in our nation. We need to learn from our partners and competitors and they also need to learn from us

It is a two- way street, and we can never live in isolation for no man can never be an island we need our partners and they need us too. In everything we do, we should know that we are competing against the world and that everyone is out there protecting and pursuing their self-interests.

This should serve as a wakeup call to us that any nation can turn their back on us any day any time henceforth, we need as many friends as we can and to stop to rely on other nations but in God and ourselves.

2. The Power of New Technology

Everyday inventions are coming into the world to make life easier and cheaper. The way we live is improving day in and day out. Forms of wealth creation are changing every day. All this being attributed to the power of new technologies that are unleashed every day. All these technologies came with the intent of making life easier for mankind and getting the job done faster.

The Hecatontagon Effect (10*10) of Transformation.

In Math a Hecatontagon is a one hundred- sided polygon and in transformation, I believe that is when a revolutionary new technology comes into play making life easier at the same time making the already existing obsolete and history.

New technologies not only unleash new wealth or make life easier for us but transform the landscape a hundred times more in what I would personally love to call the Hecatontagon Effect.

Long before the email was introduced you needed to buy an envelope, stamp, a pen, paper then put in your mailbox, later on, the postman would come to get your letter, then go to the sorting office and post the letter.

It was such a time consuming and boring process. Just imagine if you were sending the letter abroad or if you had an urgent issue that needs an immediate solution.

Thanks to the Hecatontagon Effect, we now have other functions and applications that can do the job faster for example, e-mail, Facebook, Telegram, WhatsApp, etc. These inventions have brought the world closer than ever before and you are just one click of a button away from sending your message.

So how many times more would you have sent your message faster without a postman in between? Now, these apps have come with a new reality and we have been steered into going their direction.

Let us forget about messaging apps. What about the automation of the factories and the other industries being taken over by Artificial Intelligence? These new technologies come in with a task at hand which is replacing menial tasks and minimizing costs.

We all wish we could do something about it but unfortunately, we cannot for these are laws of nature and no man can control nature. The best they can do is to make it favor them. We are in a jungle. It's either you eat, or you get eaten I pray for the former.

There is a need for us to harness the power of new technologies to our advantage to catch up with the rest of the world. If we take advantage of these new technologies, we will get to our desired destination faster than we ever thought. We can be a leading economy in Africa in one generation.

They say Rome was not built in a day we can never agree more on that aspect, but all we are saying is when Rome was built there was no Hecatontagon effect back then.

There were inferior technologies during that time for example, nothing was automated everything was manual. They did not even have power tools or discovered that you could build skyscrapers from glass and steel. We can build an empire faster than any other nation in Africa harnessing the power of new technologies.

More wealth from more innovative technologies

The 19th century was called the British century because Britain led the world in to the first Industrial Revolution. The 20th century has been called the American century for it led the world in innovation from manufacturing to information and this brought inventions like the airplane, global giants like IBM, Microsoft, Apple, GM, GE, Ford and even Hollywood.

The 21st century is also called the Chinese century, for it has seen China coming from its sleeping into a dominating force and rival to the United States. We have seen Chinese companies like Huawei, Alibaba providing unseen competition to American companies like Apple and Amazon.

There is one thing in common amongst all these giants. They all became global players not because they were born gifted more than any other nation but because of innovation.

All these nations went where there was no path created their path and left a trail there. They created new technologies and sold them to their global customers and sold them to the world and created global brands.

If one of ours gets a revelation of the future, we should not undermine them or brush them away. We never know how much money we let go of. Just come to think of the car industry, how many sub-industries were opened within one industry?

There are big companies that just focus on manufacturing car tyres for example, Goodyear and Yokohama Tyres. Some just manufacture bolts and nuts, car radios, mirrors, windshields and those who even repair cars.

Just come to think of it how many jobs are created and how much money is generated in the economy, but all this comes from one invention. Now imagine a country like America having multiple inventions like electricity, airplanes, cars and even in technology how much money could they have made for their country?

Sometimes innovations are not all about bringing something completely new, but it is about making something cooler and even simpler to use. Take Apple. for example, they did not invent the computer nor cell phones, but they simply made them cool and user-friendly by introducing the multi-touch screen technology, apps, etc.

From my understanding, I believe that Zimbabwe has not failed to make things cooler or to innovate for it has many brilliant minds for example, the boy from Murehwa who created a generator that functions with used oil.

Imagine if this invention is taken seriously how much money we would make from just selling those generators in Africa alone?

We have a young man (Sangulani Maxwell Chikumbutso) who invented the electric car that requires no charging and electric chopper that works with three different types of fuel.

The world also needs to fly or drive things that are made in Zimbabwe it is not a pipe dream it is doable. It is written in the stars that every nation is born to shine despite its disadvantages and we too can begin selling our innovations and inventions to the world.

Now is the time we begin investing in new technologies and inventing them at the same time. For no one from Mars will come and give us superficial help or ideas but our need to survive, grow and thrive should be our main motivating force.

The fact that our economy is broke, destitute with appalling living standards should give us the zeal to create inventions that make life easier, create jobs, civilize our people and also create wealth for our children.

CHAPTER THREE - LEADERSHIP REDEFINED

Leadership is that unique arrow amongst the other arrows that other arrows will always rally behind. Leadership is a big idea represented by a man followed by other men and not the other way round, of a man with a big idea followed by people.

Leadership is carrying the hopes and aspirations of those being led into one collective vision. Leadership is there to create a new path and give direction to the people.

Leadership is there to justify why people are doing something and show them what they need to do. If there is one thing that our nation needs at this moment and this hour, it's leadership!

We need leaders in our community, schools, homes, businesses but above all, we are in dire need of our national leader.

According to Dr Clare Graves, they are two tiers of leadership in a society which are The Subsistence Ethic and the Magnificence of Existence. With the former being the lowest tier and the latter being the highest and advanced order of society.

What is the Subsistence Ethic?

In a society where they use the Subsistence Ethic, the leaders just let people do what they got to do to survive. It is all about survival and following the bigger man

and not the bigger idea.

It is a society where everybody is self-enterprising for their profits and mileage. It is a society where only a few are developed, and they happen to be elites.

In such a society, people have to figure out a way themselves. It is like a home where parents take care of their children up to an age where they can fend for themselves and then leave them to find their means to survive.

The parents just make sure they give their children the basics to survive. It is a family where we just wake up doing what we have to do to put food on the table and try to make it to the next day.

This is the tier of leadership which we are using in Zimbabwe that we have all the resources we brag about having but we do not know how to use them. We want our people to have jobs because it is a basic need. We do not look at the quality and dignity of those jobs.

Our children need to go to school then we just build normal schools and not to the state -of -the-art institutions. Just because we are offering our children free education does not mean we should give them an education that is free of knowledge. Countries like German and other Nordic countries offer free education in state-of-the-art schools so why can't we do the same?

I would love to believe that our society is living on survival mode where we do not want to explore beyond what we have been exposed to or what life could offer us. Our tier of leadership is not different from the philosophy of a subsistence farmer who just farms for the sake of having food on the table and all is well after he gets enough food for his family.

He doesn't dream of living a magnificent life, being on vacation, having supercars, traveling around the world, playing golf during the weekend. Worse of all, he sets that bar as the normal life to his children and they too to grow up unexposed. This is a society that has mistaken disorder for order and the beauty of life as a luxury for to them life is all about survival and not manifesting one's greatness.

Our society is not middle-class nor goal-driven, but it is survival-driven. Therefore, immense levels of corruption and disorder are the norm because people are in the rush hour trying to catch the next train to tomorrow.

Be warned that we will never be an upper-income nation if our leadership style is survival driven but instead when it is more of a success and significance mode.

The Magnificence of Existence

In this tier people begin to care about the next person with the majority of the people being developed and exposed. Now they have passed from survival to success mode and they seek significance. They want more from what life could offer!

This a society where almost everyone has been developed, and they know how to use their resources and have a global consciousness of what exactly is happening. In such a society, people are now trying to live their purpose and fully exploit their abilities. People wake up in search of significance and to live a more fulfilling life in such a society.

This is like a family that develops their children from an early age by sending them to school mainly because they want their children to discover their purpose and live it. They make sure that wherever they send their children it's the best place where they can be to become notable members of society one day.

Our national leaders should do away with the subsistence ethic and begin to think on the lines of the magnificence of existence if we are to be an upper-income nation one day. They should begin being those parents that sacrifice their own well- being for the well- being of their children's future.

They should do away with the psychology that what they grew up doing is the best thing. They must be that kind of parent who says whatever I went through growing up I do not want my children to experience the same. All they think is *"I want my children to see the beauty of life to improve it for their children and the cycle goes on"*. They say that if you still counting on the successes of yesterday then you are a failure and leadership should learn from that.

If our leaders decide to give people jobs, they should look at the dignity of the jobs and also the quality. If they decide to build schools, they should build the best of the best institutions that will also school the best global citizens. If we move from the first tier to this tier, we can uplift the thinking, actions and even the results from our nation to that of a Higher economic state.

Inclusive Institutions

Leaders should be able to distinguish between politics and governance. Politics is a game of numbers and clout as I would love to believe governance on the other hand, is the day to day running of the country. Now what we need to do is to focus more on governance to politics.

I would like to equate politics to a game of football whereby people support different teams in one nation but when their national team is playing, they all rally behind it and support it. Now this is what we should do when it comes to the day to day running of our country.

Let's take elections as a football game between the parties we support when the match is over, we shake hands go home and attend to the major issues. The problem is that after elections we still have that election hangover and it is stagnating us from moving forward.

After elections we are usually divided into two groups and hence when our national team is playing it's already drained, and it loses its match against other foreign competitors.

Our governance is divided into partisan lines that bring nothing except hate, retrogression and economic quagmire. When elections are over or even if the party, we do not support gets power we should put that aside becoming one team towards building a strong and resilient nation.

Our model of governance should include everyone as a stakeholder and not be extractive by giving only a few entitlements as shareholders in our country. We all want to be part of the process of building our country, but no one wants to be part of something they feel like they have no total control and are not part of the decision making. We all feel motivated if we are counted on than counted out.

In my own eyes there is no hypocrisy that beats a man whose actions are different from his words. Our integration should not be on paper nor in our mouths only but also our actions.

If we claim to be inclusive let us build a model that is inclusive and quickly eulogize our extractive institutions.

It is also time we start having a national vision and not party visions. A national vision is not only enacted by the governing party but by all stakeholders for it affects everyone. Political parties should know that they are not there in governance to protect the agenda of the party but the national agenda.

The role of the government is to create a conducive environment for social enterprise for every citizen. Also, the government exists to promote and foster unity amongst its citizens in everything it does and initiates. A, national vision should be crafted beyond the governing party to the extent that anyone could drive the vision in case the existing government fails.

This is the job of every government to rally the people as its stakeholders towards one motivational vision. It is a huge problem when everyone wants to take solo credit and give it to their party to gain political mileage.

This will bring nothing to our country except for divide, harm and retrogression as we have seen in the previous years. If we do not create inclusive institutions, then we are digging our own grave into the future. No country was ever an economic powerhouse, political powerhouse or even a cultural powerhouse because of its divisions.

For us to claim our power in the future, we need to create inclusivity in our stakeholders from a very young age. We need to do away with political divisions, tribalism and a divide of, race, color and religion.

To remove tribalism, we need to start teaching Ndebele, Shona, and English as compulsory in our country. We need to create a cultural identity as a country that is inclusive of all the people in the country.

Our vehicle into the future needs to leave no willing Zimbabwean behind due to their political affiliation, age, nor gender. It should be big enough to carry us all to our desired and born to be the destination of greatness.

Therefore, it is of utmost importance that all leaders build an inclusive state because it is not only motivational but also will make us stronger as a nation. We have been fragmented for too long leaving us with nothing except for hatred and retrogression as a nation and now we have become a failed state.

We should learn from history, the mistakes of our predecessors and one of the biggest mistakes, ever to happen in our governance was the building of an extractive to an inclusive state from the beginning. I guess we cannot go back to the start and change the beginning, but we can change the direction of our vehicle to change the ending.

Our Model of Governance

One of the greatest mistakes that many nations have made in particular African ones, is an ideological straitjacket approach. This is the thinking that if you are aligned with the West you would be a capitalist nation by default. If you were aligned to the East, you would become more of a Socialist.

African leaders became chauvinists because they started following their friends' ideologies for *"political honesty"* in the eyes of their people. It is not about who your friend or enemy is. We must apply what applies to our present-day situation despite where it comes from.

No system can never work alone for systems are designed to be interconnected I believe that systems are interdependent like the human body and if one part of the human body is cut out you become disabled and the same applies to our systems of governance.

Communism nor Socialism, democracy and capitalism alone can never be perfect in a country, for these systems have stages and can complement one another. Who says that a country can only be a democratic nation without socialist elements in it or a country can only be a socialist country without enterprising elements in it to create and distribute wealth in a democratic way?

Do we have a perpetual contract with only one system of governance? No one will ever tax us or imprison our nation because of applying what is applicable in our country.

China saw this problem under Deng Xiaoping that their ideological straitjacket approach had brought nothing to a sleeping giant apart from poverty, isolation from the world and economic quandary.

Their approach was rather the creation of *"Socialism with Chinese characteristics."* which saw them rise within a limited amount of time into a global giant. We cannot abandon our cultural identity nor force a system that will not suit our realties. We have a lot of pros we can get from Socialism, Communism, Capitalism and Democracy.

We can create a state with positive socialist, communist, capitalist and democratic elements and no one can never stop us. Together as a people and as a nation we can change this failed concept of governance that has been in our country for quite a long time. Of course, we cannot re-invent the wheel but instead of what has been invented we can find another way home from the already existing roads and as a result of interlinking the roads we can create a new map.

We are not the first country to try and create a favorable framework of governance that favors its stakeholders so we should not be afraid to do so. Let us move away from being that student that copies everything word for word and even the name of the person whom they are copying from.

This not only disqualifies that student but also makes you lose your identity as a person. That is what ideological straitjacket approach looks like we not only lose our identity to our "friends" whom we try to mimic but also disqualifies us from the game before it even starts.

Like what Deng Xiaoping said to his fellow CCP comrades in one of his addresses that *"We do have friends, but we do cherish our freedom"*. Please be reminded that our freedom needs to be cherished by implementing what's favorable to our people and what our freedom fighters died for.

I am not saying we should sideline *"friends"* or those who want to assist nevertheless we should create boundaries for them in the day to day running of our national affairs. No matter what Zimbabwe belongs to Zimbabweans; (at home and abroad, the born and even the unborn) therefore their sovereignty and interests should be protected in whatever decision that is made.

At the same time, we can also learn one or two things from our *"so-called enemies"* and *"friends"* (competitors) on what we could do to build our country. We are free to choose what system to use in our country but at the same time we are obliged to protect and defend the interests of the Zimbabwean child before opening our door to the outside world.

Visionary Leadership

"The future belongs to the one who sees it first and acts on it."

It is universal wisdom that without a vision, the people will perish. A bus without a destination can never go anywhere. Vision is what separates the lions and the sheep, the boys and men above all the leaders and the followers.

Like what nutrition is to the body so is a vision to leadership is it is essential that gives leadership life. Leadership is like a diet that requires balanced constituents and for it to be balanced the meal can never be complete without the vision being served on the plate.

If a nation is run by a visionless leadership, it is not only ripe for failure but utter destruction. A leader's vision can be for good or for the worse in a nation. Just imagine Hitler's vision for Germany to have the *"pure"* Aryan race running Germany.

This had disastrous effects on the minorities especially the Jews who ended up falling victim to the Holocaust. Now, look at JFK's vision to land a man on the moon by the end of the decade (1960's) which ended up happening despite his death.

The common factor here is both these visions had an impact on the world that is still being felt up to now. The major difference is that one impacted the world for better and inspired other nations to follow suit. Then the other one made the world bitter and sent the world into a war with disastrous effects still being felt up to the present day.

The reason why JFK's moon mission ended up being successful was that it was an inclusive national vision that was bigger than him as a president but indebted to the nation. That is why even six years after his death a man landed on the moon.

The reason why Hitler's vision never lived beyond but behind him was because it was self-centered, selfish and cruel, besides that no one wanted to carry on a cruel and selfish legacy.

That is the power of a vision it creates a better world or destroys the already existing system for the worst.

The greatest leaders of all time: from the religious ones like Jesus Christ, Prophet Muhammad (S.A.W), emperors like Julius Caesar, Alexander the Great to business leaders like Steve Jobs, Bill Gates, Lee Iacocca and even civil leaders like Gandhi and Dr. King all had a vision that they woke up in pursuit of every-day.

But a vision can never be greater or move beyond its architect if it lacks its building blocks.

What are the building blocks of a vision?

This is a vision that has got a future picture of what is of the future that it intends to achieve. It is a vision aided by the conduct of ethics and behavioral processes on how to achieve the vision. They also comprise the right budget towards financing the vision into a reality. Finally, the vision should also consist of a clear, concise, clear plan of how to turn the vision into a tangible reality.

Future Picture

A leader 's vision should sell an imaginable future picture that we the people feel part of. For example, in our case we have failed to imagine a clear picture of the future together. We haven't had a picture of the future of what our beloved nation would look like in the next generation.

We all want and hope for the best for our nation, but our leaders haven't given us a picture of Zimbabwe except the reason to give up dreaming. All our hope has been lost and we are too busy to dream of what exactly Zimbabwe could be apart from dreaming how the world would be if we were never born in Zimbabwe.

Our faith has been tested and our hope in our nation has been lost simply because we don't have an end in mind of what exactly we want to achieve, simply put we do not know what exactly it is we want as a nation.

We are drained of our energy because we have no future picture, so we are not motivated to pursue anything but rather it's demotivating. We need to start having an imaginable vision that moves us all into the future.

Sufficient Funding

For us to achieve our vision as a nation we need to have an adequate budget for us to finance that vision. Even the moon mission had its budget for it to turn from an aspiration into a vision and later into a success story. Like I once equated a vision into a journey, no journey will ever be embarked on without adequate money for the journey or without budgeting money to finance the trip.

Either it will always be a dream journey, or you end up not going where you wanted to be in the first place. If our vision is not backed by an adequate budget it will always remain an impending project due to capital constraints.

Many leaders come into office with a very good vision like building very great empires but instead they leave office without building anything or half-way through the project.

No matter how hard they try to communicate their vision or pursue it despite all the energy they fail. It is because the vision is not complete; it is weak it is missing part of its backbone which is an adequate budget.

It has been done before by other nations and we can learn from them on what they did to raise funds to finance their megaprojects. It is not a scary process nor rocket science for we have the resources both natural and human resources to help us get these funds.

We just have to align our resources in such a way that we become irresistible to attract the capital we need to be where we want to go. There is a lot of money on the free market waiting for places to go and to be invested in.

Like Adam Smith in the Wealth of Nations, that *"money is an instrument of commerce,"* hence we need it to make things happen in our nation because it is an enabling tool. For that reason, our vision will never be a reality but an aspiration if it does not account for an adequate budget.

Value Systems

You can be the greatest leader with one of the greatest visions that the world has ever seen but you are at the risk of becoming another Hitler if you do not have an ethical code on your behavioral processes as to how you shall achieve your vision. Many leaders have achieved a lot but without really being critical of how their organizations and nations achieve their goals. If there is a paradigm that has destroyed leaders is the thinking that *"we shall achieve our goal by any means necessary"*.

This forces people to go astray with their values towards achieving material success if it means manipulating people they do so and even if it means through killing and stealing, they will do so. It is a thinking that has destroyed our moral fiber as people, as nations and even as organizations. This only makes people lesser than material with profitability put before principles, the planet and the people.

If we are to fight the corruption that we claim to be fighting in our nation, we should not just address it by the mouth but through action. We need to stop having double standards about corruption like what it is today that when corruption favors you, you claim to have *"connections"* and when it does not favor you call it corruption. We must not be a nation of hypocrites and pretenders for us to achieve whatever we want materially. Our vision can never be complete if we lose our ethics towards us achieving our goals.

History has taught us that even the Global giants came to fall because of poor ethics. Take Enron for example, it fell because of the lack of ethics and quick fixes to make profits as soon as they could.

This was all by putting profits before people and the planet leaving behind unhealed wounds and scars that have cost many families up to this day. We are tasked to build bridges between profits and principles, what we shall achieve and how we achieve it.

As much we have permanent interests, we also have a permanent mandate which is to protect our people and our country. This should be our greatest imperative when building a sustainable economy, nation and a *"Gentle"* empire.

If we fail to include values in our vision, we will be creating a catastrophic legacy for our future generations. It is our duty and mandate to build bridges between our vision and values. It is our task to find a way to make profits and principles co-relate if we are to position Zimbabwe in its future place of leading Africa in the next generation.

The Strategic Plan

If a vision has no strategic plan to execute it then it is an all-show no-go rocking horse. It will remain an aspiration and wishful thinking that will never become a reality.

Having a great vision without a strategic plan is like digging your way into your own grave. If a country does not have its strategic plan for the next 30-60 years be assured that it is leaving nothing apart from poverty, debt and impending projects for its future stakeholders.

A strategy is like a nation's competitive advantage over its rivals and if it does not have any strategic plan then it becomes easy prey to the big predators of Globalization. If you do not know your route and your mode of transport to get to your destination you are going to get lost

In this scenario, no one will come to your aid for they do not know where you want to go. Presumably you get lucky and they come, they might come with good intentions but if a map or route is not provided, how do you expect to get where you want to be?

As the famous adage goes, *"We are captains of our ships and masters of our fate"* therefore, no ship captain takes control of the wheel without knowing the route towards their intended destination.

If we do not have a strategy, we can be fooled into pursuing anything that will see us regress. Often, we blame the foreign powers both the East and the West for our misfortune under the guise that we are being exploited.

Almost every politician has created a critical mass from either blaming China or the USA for our country's misfortune. I am not supporting exploitation, but we too are to blame because we do not have a plan for our country.

Complaining, politicking, and whining is never a strategy for us to achieve our vision, there is an adage that says, *"your goals do not care about how you feel today"*. Yes, we are a down-trodden people, we have been let down as we may want to put it.

If we do not have a strategy to lift ourselves, then we shall remain downtrodden until Christ's second coming but do not forget that even the scriptures say, *"God helps those who help themselves."*

If we do not create a vision without its strategic visionary components which are the future picture, strategic plan, adequate budget and value systems it will just be an academic document full of wishful thinking that will leave a tainted legacy for future generations.

Openness to Ideas

If someone argues or criticizes you, it does not make them your enemy, but it is just their opinion and outlook towards things. I believe that scholars like to call it a different school of thought.

People are not fighting nor following anyone due to what is in a politician's head, but they follow where they can get material benefits. The citizens of this beloved nation called Zimbabwe are not fighting for the level of intellectual capacity their leaders have but for a better life.

Criticizing the government for the benefit of the common citizen does not make one an enemy of the state. If the citizens keep quiet, they are to blame because they become their enemies and enemies of progress. The government should be able to classify between an enemy, friend and strategic visionary partner in the country.

If one proposes something, it does not mean that they are aligned to the opposition or they want to subvert the government. Even if the opposition opposes the government, it should also work as a partner in developing the country and as a shadow government of the current government.

We can never run the country with one idea overshadowing the other who said it is the norm and who said it is correct? Jan Phillips, in her book The Art of Original Thinking: The Making of a Thought Leader says, *"If we find two opposing sides, we* do not pick up a side, but we find a way to make both co-exist."

Nation-building is not war nor a battlefield of ideas hence we do not pick a side, but we integrate our ideas into one powerful synergy. We are not saying that this country should be a one-party state no, but we are advocating for politics that unifies our country and not that which divides it.

Democracy is not only a multi-party state but also a marketplace of ideas where ideas are honored and respected. If we undermine and prevent ideas from those not in government, we are not preventing ideas, but we are preventing the progress of our society.

Imagine if America was to prevent Bill Gates, the Wright Brothers, Steve Jobs and the Jeff Bezos, where would they be today in terms of progress? We are nowhere near to the promised land if we continue to undermine ideas and to prevent them from being executed. Instead, we are near to us seeing the end of our nation before the world even comes to an end if we continue like this.

Simply put we are digging our own grave and creating a tainted legacy for future generations. Henceforth, both leaders from the leading and opposing parties should not shy away from ideas that promote national development because of the insecurities guided by fearing their loss of power.

Leaders should not feel threatened by ideas but instead they should feel empowered and strengthened by them. We are not saying that leaders should implement every idea that comes into their way, but they should be at least open to them. They cannot apply all and please all but certainly, they should appeal to the majority. Leaders should apply what applies to our realities, culture and norms.

Even if our leaders have good intentions when they ascend to positions of power, they can fail on their first day in office if the diet of the leadership is not balanced. If our leadership lacks essential nutrients like strategic visionary architecture, building inclusive institutions, the second tier of leadership and openness to ideas, they are building nothing apart from a pariah -state.

It is imperative leaders understand the magnitude of the task that lies ahead of them and that the future of the nation relies on their understanding, wisdom, worldviews and actions.

To the leaders of Zimbabwe, the present and future leaders; the choice is all yours, the fate of this country depends on you and how you embrace and see your task.

CHAPTER FOUR - ENGAGING A PARADIGM SHIFT

If there is one thing that we ought to do as a nation is to do away with old processes and thinking, for example, colonial inertia, the war rhetoric, the academic syndrome, etc. These are old myths, and they are no longer going to drive us anywhere but instead keep us stuck.

Almost every nation if not all nations fought wars of Independence, but they are done with that rhetoric for that was the struggle of that time. As Franz Fanon says that *"each generation must out of its relative obscurity find its mission fulfill it or betray it,"* our founding fathers had to free this country from white minority rule and our task is to wage an economic revolution.

Every nation is not a finished product but still in the process of construction and every day it is being constructed to be habitable for its citizens. Our founding fathers ran their race, left where they could and now it is time for us the youth to run our race which is economic transformation.

Personally, I am saddened by an ancient school of thought that believes that the younger people are not patriotic enough, mature enough and they don't appreciate where we are coming from as a nation. This paradigm fails to allude to the fact that the younger people are the ones who will be the parents in the next generation and the ones who will inherit this country.

The other thing is that the war rhetoric has become a cliché in our society. It is now losing its value to the young for it is used every-day and they feel like they do not get anything from it. You cannot tell someone to appreciate their history when the present is so uncertain, and the future looks so bleak. The young do appreciate the efforts, they are also patriotic and energetic to move their country to the best place it can ever be.

Mind you we are in the 21st century other nations are talking about the Fourth Industrial Revolution and how they can create wealth for their nations 40 years from now and we were talking about our achievements 40 years ago. When those same nations come into our country selling their newly discovered technologies, we feel like we are being robbed of our wealth and exploited. Truth be told, we are just sitting on our potential and celebrating the successes of 40 years back.

China's economy grew 70 times plus in those forty years' big companies like Apple and Microsoft were still startups now they are tech giants. Google wasn't even founded back then now it's even bigger than our economy and we are still hung-over to that one accolade we have won the *"WAR"*

Colonial Inertia

We are continuing with processes and institutions that were built during colonial times. What we fail to understand is that the colonial model was successful to the minority that their leaders represented and not the majority. The white minority saw the magnificence of existence and the majority were just surviving.

That is the reason why the majority still struggles today because the model we still have in existence is just a continuation of what was left by the Smith regime. We have many graduates that come from our schools' especially tertiary institutions with higher qualifications, but some are vendors and just informally employed.

This is because of this system that was meant to benefit only a few who thought that they had a divine right to be prosperous more than others. Back then, the African people mainly worked in blue-collar jobs, and the white-collar jobs were reserved mainly for the minority and the system was structured in such a system that it only benefits them.1980 came then most of the white people left the newly founded nation of Zimbabwe.

The few Africans who were elites moved into jobs that were left by the white people and bought houses in leafy suburbs that the white people used to own. Ever since independence, we did not create any new industries or found any big companies that were to offer jobs to the graduating students from tertiary institutions and even high schools both the blue and white-collar jobs.

We were enjoying the benefits of our independence, our inheritance, along the way we forgot to build new institutions even revolutionizing and expanding the already existing industries to increase the carrying capacity to include the majority.

Yes, they were places and institutions that we tried our best and I personally applause that for example, in our education sector when we built more state-owned universities and colleges. But an important element that was left is giving elite education to all and not just finding elite education in private institutions.

If we want to build a great Zimbabwe that benefits us, we ought to dunk and sink colonial inertia for we do not owe anything to it and the road to heaven does not pass through its house. Because we have failed to do away with colonial inertia people have become so nostalgic about the past as the best life, they will ever live, and they want to go back to the *"golden-days"*.

Academic Syndrome

The bottleneck education system was designed during colonial times to keep the Africans out of governance and policymaking. The colonialists were a bit smart about keeping Africans out of the system by destroying their organic and divine makeup.

They created the bottleneck education system under the guise of *"education is the key to success"* that without schooling you were just a spectator in the community. Only a few Africans were destined to make it to the top and they would win the respect of their fellow brothers and sisters by becoming lawyers, teachers, doctors and nurses.

It was even a pre-requisite for one to be ''educated'' to be able to vote in selecting a government of choice. Now we have excluded many ''un-educated'' people who are naturally gifted in what they are doing because of the continuation of the bottleneck system that made us cram, pass, forget then make it to the top.

It was a system that murdered our divine and organic intellectual thinking, instead, it made us fight against it to be respected by having our value on paper.

After independence we raced into schools expecting to make it if we were academics and became too academic and ignored the divine and organic make up. We were left with the thinking that the more time you spend in school, the smarter you become, and you can solve problems faster than those that did not go to school. Now this thinking is being passed on from generation to generation and every day we are producing more people with Masters and PhDs.

With the level in which we are moving, a bachelor's degree will be equivalent to Advanced Level in the near future and people will keep on going to school just to maintain the score by earning master's and PHDs. It is a race to get to the top of the bottle and make it out.

We shall have more scholastic doctors and a few solutions in our country because we were left with the thinking that without school, we are nothing. The misconception here was that we confuse schooling with education, and we opted to be schooled and not to be educated.

Unfortunately, with the Fourth Industrial Revolution and big companies like Apple, Google, Amazon amongst others claiming that they will not require a bachelor's degree as a prerequisite for one to work for them. The 21st century requires one to have soft skills, which are leadership, teamwork, creativity and work ethic.

As Alvin Toffler says, *"the illiterate of the 21st century will not be those who cannot read and write, but those who cannot learn, unlearn and relearn"*. Our country needs to learn to recognize those with soft skills for they are not taught in school, but they are divine and more organic.

If you look at people like Thomas Edison a man with over two thousand plus patents in his name, he was sacked from school at the age of ten because teachers said he was too stupid to teach.

People like Steve Jobs, Bill Gates, Michael Dell and Larry Ellison were all university dropouts, but they made an impact on modern-day technology. The reason why they dropped out of university is not that school is stupid but that they never found what they were looking for, instead, they had to leave and go look for it in the universe.

Imagine how much these men have contributed to the economy of their country and in other countries. If our nation could learn from this that genius does not mean going to school and creativity is not taught there it is something that is born within.

The same way we respect academics is the same way we should also respect those with soft skills for we need them, and they also have a greater role to play in society. If we do not want to be an illiterate nation of the 21st century, it is high time we begin to unlearn and relearn by engaging a new perspective into the future by rethinking our future, crushing old processes and re-creating value.

CHAPTER FIVE - A NEW REALITY IS BORN

At school we were taught that colonialism brought in three R's into our country which was Reading, Writing and Arithmetic making Africans literate and handy to the white man.

Now it is no longer the 19th century it is now the 21st-century memorizing information, mental arithmetic and all have been made easier by new tools like the internet, calculators, functions like Google-Talk and Siri on our phones that we can all tell what to do and we can get the answer faster.

Almost everyone can read or write and to most it is no longer a big deal it is now an involuntary action like breathing. Welcome, to the 21st century, no matter how many degrees you have or how much experience you have, if you can-not be organic enough to imagine the new, crush the old and create the value you will always be an illiterate nation.

This a century of innovation and new technologies, a century of re-creation, re-creation and the process will keep on going on till the earth comes to an end. In this day and age if we relax on the edge of our seats, we will always be victims of a system that we never created but if we are paranoid and creative enough, we will be beneficiaries of our creation. In this chapter, I am going to introduce three concepts that I borrow from Hannington Mubaiwa which are:

Re-Engineering, Re-Imagineering and Re-Entrepreneuring and I describe them in my own words.

Below is a self-explanatory Transformational Re-Engineering Map designed by professor Hannington Mubaiwa showing and explaining the re-structuring process from rethinking new ideas to the institutionalization of the ideas. What we can all see and perhaps learn, and practice is that everything can be broken down to science. If there is one thing that my professor emphasized is the idea that I must always first look for the natural way of doing things. I must look for the scientific principles which underly the best way of achieving the best possible results. Is our government working the science?

Below is a diagram designed by Hannington Mubaiwa showing the Re-Engineering process in creating a new vision and designing a new process into the future.

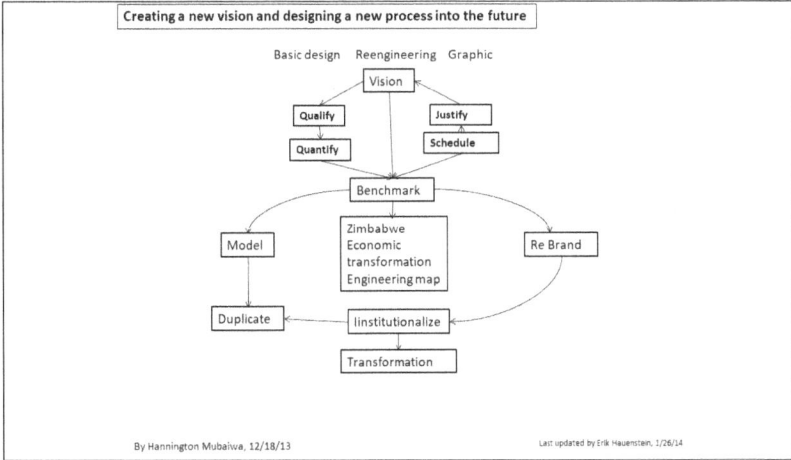

Creating a new vision and designing a new process into the future

By Hannington Mubaiwa, 12/18/13   Last updated by Erik Hauenstein, 1/26/14

Rethinking Zimbabwe

A paradigm shift requires nothing apart from a new thought process which is completely new. We need new radical thinking that completely shakes the status quo that will bring in a new reality. It is time we employ new thinking for Zimbabwe that is completely different from the one that we already have.

Away with the thinking that we are a downtrodden people who will never reach Canaan, that we are down forever and that there is no light at the end of the tunnel! As Hannington Mubaiwa states *"Wherever you are going to be in life twenty years from now physically it is determined by where you are today mentally"*.

Wherever we are going to be tomorrow it starts today from the mental picture we have in our heads today and we should always start our journey with an end in mind. Once we start walking with a new picture of the future in our heads one day it will become a revelation. We will certainly bump into what we exactly have in our heads physically one day.

We need a new idea to drive us into the future. We need new myths to drive us into the future, a new myth that will live beyond us, a new myth of our time and a new myth of all time. Many, successful nations are driven by mental pictures full of myths and ideas which they all wake up in search of physically. They have national dreams which they want to turn into a reality.

A myth is an accepted lie that can be passed on from generation to generation and it becomes part of the culture of the people. For instance, America has promoted a myth that has been passed on from generation to generation which is the American Dream that; America is a place where dreams come true.

Even the world has been bought into believing it to the extent that the crème de la crème of many nations strives every-day to get into the Land of Bold and The Brave, a land where dreams come true.

Around the world people take SATs, ACTs to get in any college in America so that they have a feel of what it feels like dreaming the American Dream. It is because America is moving and has always moved with a mental picture which became a revelation to the world.

Who says we cannot have our idea, our myth that will make us a destination and envy of the rest of the world? What stops us from having people from the world from coming to Zimbabwe to learn and buy properties in Kariba or Victoria Falls.

If we all come to think of it, Dubai a city-state, that was once a desert barely forty years ago today its skyline is breath-taking and now it has become the envy of the world. It all came from a dream, an idea that one day the world would come to them.

Even Singapore came from nothing into something today it is an economic miracle all these are examples of hope and inspiration. In the 80s China said they wanted to quadruple their economy by 2002 and they reached their goal two years later in 2004. Today China is a super-power and a giant of the 21st century.

We should start thinking of Zimbabwe as an African superpower, a destination for the world, a consumer capital of Africa, the financial center of Africa and even the Industrial hub for Africa. The good thing about having an idea or a dream is that no-one taxes you for having a dream.

No one will arrest us for having an image of what our country could be. The worst they could do to discourage us is by telling us that it is wishful thinking and we cannot achieve it because we are a poor nation now.

The truth is we are not poor we are just broke; we do not have indigenous capital access, but it is not a limiting factor after the idea starts manifesting itself. We should not worry about that for when the idea is powerful it will become magnetic enough to attract the resources that it needs both human and capital.

Hannington Mubaiwa says *"When you start moving the things, the places and the people will start moving with you"* but you should move with a picture, an idea with you then the universe will send people and even money to make it a reality.

Whatever we aspire to be and whatever we have dreamt of becoming we can become it all starts in our imagination. Whatever we aspire to be it is already there we just have to walk into its existence, it is the universe telling us to go claim our place in the future even without anything we shall get something along the way.

Pablo Picasso says *"So long as you can imagine it, it is real"* so whatever we dream of having in this nation we shall possess. The author says; *"Reality is imagination brought to life for everything that we have around us started as imagination for that is why they say, things that are were created from things that are not".*

From this day forward, our tomorrow reality of Zimbabwe will come to pass when we re-think it today from where we are already to where we want to be in the future.

Destroying the Old

After we have imagined our new future it is quite imperative for us to unlearn old habits and processes that we were married to in the past. They say success is a habitual process it has to do with your daily habits.

If we want a successful future, we can't continue having bad practices, habits and expect the best of results we will die with imagination in our heads. We cannot afford to go the grave with dead ghosts within us that were never brought to life because of our bad habits. We cannot afford to leave a tainted legacy of impending projects, debts, and a failed state to our children all this being indebted to poor old and archaic moribund habits.

It is utter insanity for us to use the same methods and expect some miraculous and super motivating results. There, is no negotiation about this one we totally have to crush old processes and we need not be apologetic about it. Sometimes when your house is ruined all you ought to do is to destroy it to its foundation and allow the building of a new one.

If we all come to think of it, death is the common denominator for us all it is part of life. It is paradoxically the end and the beginning of everything meaning that as the other life ends another one begins.

That is why most of us believe in *"Life After Death"* the promise of Heaven and Hell, the belief in reincarnation and that is why in ancient times Egyptian kings were mummified for people believed that they would start a new life after they die.

In Transformation and science, we call it metamorphosis whereby death is necessary for the creation of a new life like the fading away of the ugly caterpillar into something new a beautiful butterfly.

We should take the process of metamorphosis as a positive process for we are just burying an old ailing uncle and the next day we are having a new beautiful, energetic, powerful and full-of-potential baby in the house.

That is the beauty of bidding farewell to our old methods for new ones come in with a promise of a new, hopeful, beautiful energetic future for us and those coming behind us. Everything has a life cycle according to science; from people, animals, ideas and even nations that is destiny. They all start at gestation till they all reach a point of saturation then they die.

We can try to prevent death by delaying it or living longer but it will certainly come. Just imagine that before Galileo Galilee came into existence the world believed that the sun revolved around the earth and until he changed the thinking that resulted in him being convicted.

He was convicted because people were in denial of what was perceived as conventional wisdom that had been passed on from generation unto generation had been challenged. Whenever our loved ones who happen to be so dear to our heart pass on, we live in denial for the first time when the message hits us but as time goes on, we fully start transitioning to living without them.

Change is a constant and often we are so resistant to it for it shakes and challenges what we already know. Often, we see it as our enemy and declare war on it or whoever is leading it. We cannot just let go of what we have been taught, what we have been exposed to. Mainly because we are now experts and we are convinced that there is no other way and we are on the right path.

Go into any office of any high-level person, present something new, they say *"been there done that, we have high-level technocrats and experts working on it"* then if you go back to them exactly a year later nothing has been done! Why? Because we fear change and we are driven by the fear of loss more than the potential of gain.

The answer is we have become experts in our processes forgetting that these are the same processes that brought us here where we are, and we want to use them to move us from where we are. We have convinced ourselves that we know it all and that it is the universal truth unfortunately we should be able to classify amongst the truth and experts' opinions.

An expert's opinion is just one's conviction over issues they are exposed to due to their experiences in a certain field. Then truth is an embodiment of facts that are believed to be true universally.

A mechanic can tell you that if a car begins to produce a squeaky sound from the engine it is a new timing belt that is needed that is an expert's opinion and not the truth. When you are told that what is left after birth is death, we all know that we are going to die, and this is truth everyone is born, and everyone dies.

Our old processes have reached a stage of saturation, they are exhausted, they need to be retired for they are no longer competent for the job anymore and some of them were even a menace either way.

If we do not pick up the bad apples from the basket the whole basket will be contaminated, and we will be forced to throw the whole basket away. This is the greatest challenge we face at this hour that if we do not crash and thrash bad habits, we will be crying foul soon for it is going to be a disaster for us.

As the adage goes *"fortune favors the brave"*, it is not merely the ones with the bravery of confronting the biggest elephant in the room but also those with the courage to let go of what they used to do before.

History has proven to us that we have had many old processes that have been passed on from generation to generation that have mislead us over the past years and its time we break away from the yoke. We might have been told that history repeats itself, but it will do so when we do not take action as a people.

Remember politicians are human too, stop idolizing them.

This is an impediment that has arrested us from generation unto generation, we have put so much faith in politicians and seeing them as demi-gods. We have been molded into seeing politicians as messiahs as if they are like the modern-day Hercules sent into the world by Zeus with special powers.

We have been arrested in the thinking that without a politician no change would come to our country. We always at rallies chanting slogans that do not bring any development but instead dividing our country. We idolize politicians to the extent that their names become larger than life and they become the institutions, government and even the vision.

We have been groomed to follow the big man as a substitute for the big idea because of their charisma and we cannot even question them for if we do so we perceived as enemies. It is a sickness that needs a quicker remedy for it is contagious, the generations to come are at risk of being contaminated too and it will lead us nowhere except into a failed state.

If a concerned citizen gives a proposition they are quickly categorized as enemies of change and progress or a member of the other party because a politician will be at risk of losing political grip and a following.

That culture of not questioning and not challenging those we trust with a public office or who aspire to be must be stopped. We should accept that we are all human beings, we all make mistakes and we should not feel threatened if our counterparts give us ideas.

We should be able to question those who lead and they should also realize that they are human and make mistakes too. If the sailors of a ship, see that the ship is about to sink they are allowed to inform the captain about their fate if not they will all sink both the captain and the sailors indiscriminately.

We should be able to understand that politicians and our leaders do not have all the answers they are not God so we should not be afraid and must be able to confront them when things go wrong. Correcting our leaders does not mean we hate them but that we are just skeptical about our future and we are just trying to avoid a shipwreck which they might not be seeing.

The people also should not become robots who do not question the intentions of our leaders and only giving praises to their demagogic speeches and populist agendas.

We should know that the real reason why the Titanic sank was because of a ship-owner who put his ego ahead of the lives of the passengers for he wanted to break records and feature in the papers which ended up in the tragedy that left many dead.

In this we learn that leaders should always do the right thing and not the popular thing just for the sake of clout and fame.

Robert Mugabe ended up staying in power longer than he should have been and left a tainted legacy because his charisma earned him the title of a demi-god; one who had been sent by God as the only liberator of the people. After the liberation struggle people celebrated at the same time relaxed and gave him dominion power over them and that's when the demagogue nature began until his demise.

We should always learn from history for it is not only our past, but it determines our present and future. In the process of idolizing politicians, we become convinced that our world revolves around them and that they are the shareholders of our change process. I think we forget that we the people are the creators and authors of our destiny.

We forget that politicians build no industries but we the citizens do so, and they have to create a strong support system and a conducive environment for social enterprise.

Name any nation that was built by politicians alone without the help and hand of its citizens. Look at the USA for example, people like Carnegie, Rockefeller, Vanderbilt, Scott, J.P Morgan, Edison and Ford were not politicians.

Look at Japan and people like the Konusike Matsushitas and the Hondas etc. Were all these men politicians?

I am not saying politicians are irrelevant but instead we are saying we desist from surrendering our all to them that are selling ourselves and our abilities to them in exchange for empty promises and *"hope"*.

Why are we languishing in a jail cell when the prison gates are open? Why have we been confined to thinking that politicians breathe flavored oxygen and are different from us?

Who said we could not question their intentions as a people? Let us start to see beyond what has been presented in our eyes and go beyond in pursuit of what works for us.

The Dependence Syndrome

Below is a diagram with a concept that I borrowed from Hannington Mubaiwa which is called *"Spinning the African"* showing how Africa has been kept under illusions and myths by the *"International Community"* under the impression that they will uplift us from the mud.Ironically they make the mud and spinus to think they are the solution.

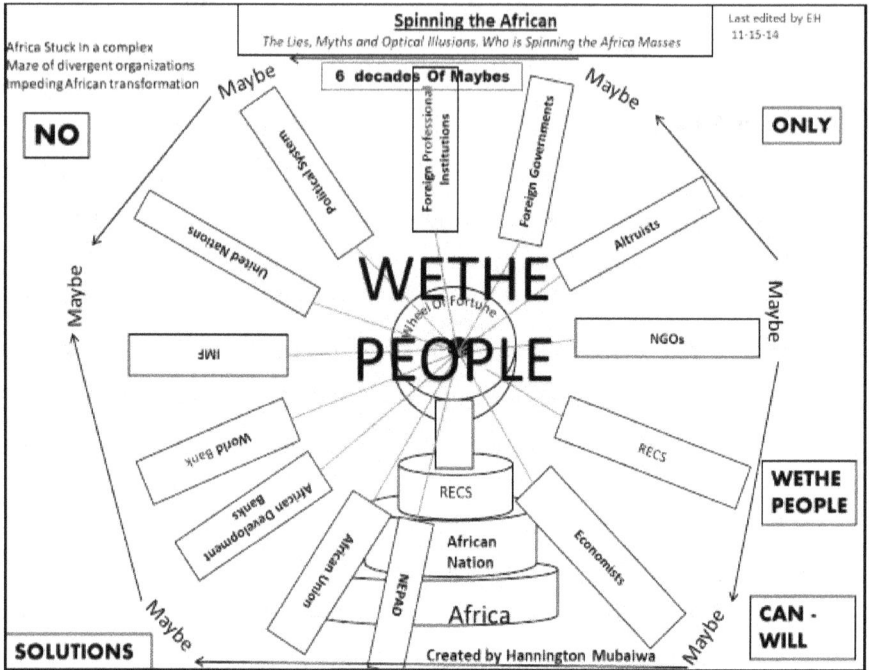

Spinning the African
The Lies, Myths and Optical Illusions. Who is Spinning the Africa Masses

Last edited by EH 11-15-14

Africa Stuck in a complex Maze of divergent organizations Impeding African transformation

6 decades Of Maybes

NO

ONLY

Maybe

Maybe

Maybe

Foreign Professional Institutions

Foreign Governments

Political System

United Nations

Altruists

WETHE PEOPLE

Wheel Of Fortune

IMF

NGOs

Maybe

Maybe

World Bank

RECS

WETHE PEOPLE

African Development Banks

RECS

African Union

NEPAD

African Nation

Economists

CAN - WILL

SOLUTIONS

Maybe

Africa

Maybe

Created by Hannington Mubaiwa

If there are other delusion and sickness that has murdered us as a nation it is the Dependence Syndrome, we think that the International community shall come in one day and solve our problems for us out of their "kindness" and mercy.

We have begun to think that someone will come from Mars, endorse what we are doing and that is the day we prosper. The saddest thing is that day will never come and that is destiny, but the good thing is we create our destiny.

We think that we shall rebuild our country out of the benevolence of the British, American, French and Chinese taxpayers' money. Our syndrome has gotten to the point that we sleep over our situation and think that other nations lose sleep over our situation too.

What we are doing is we are expecting a ship at an airport. We are living a fairytale life that of Sleeping Beauty who slept the longest until she was woken up by Prince Charming, we are sleeping, sitting and relying on *"Prince Savior"* to come and help us.

Day in day out we are looking for ways in which we can increase our approval ratings from the "International community'' in our national affairs and forgetting the main thing which is building our country.

Even our political parties all preach the same doctrine boasting of having friends amongst the *"International community"* and we think that those are the ones who will bring the meaningful change we can all count on.

Do these nations lose sleep worrying about what we think of them? Do they even consult us when they have a major project they want to initiate? We tend to forget that they too are nations with problems like us, they too are human beings like us and not more human and that whatever they implement it is a matter of what suits their needs in their nations.

We should stop moving in a façade of wanting to be them for we will never be them. We need to find our own identity economically, socially and even culturally. When we are hungry, we eat do we ask anyone for permission to eat our food? No, I believe it is just an issue of instincts and needs. As Zimbabweans when we feel as if we want to do something, let us do it we are enough for it and we should not be intimidated and feel as if we need approval from anyone.

Innovation and inventions in our country should be an involuntary process like breathing, it just happens when you are alive for that is where life comes from. It is an inalienable right that should not be taken away from us. If our creativity fades, we die as a nation.

Why would you choose to feed on the breadcrumbs when the bread is there? Till when shall we continue being on the receiving end of donor aid and subsidies to keep our economy surviving?

We were not born innately incapable of being a great nation we are just scared of trying the new!

Imagine the day we face our Creator and we are questioned before Him why we failed to utilize our resources and then we say, *"we were scared!"* I am afraid that the answer won't be sufficient enough because we were given divine powers on earth and dominion over everything.

The only power that we lack is the ability to raise the dead and bring them back to the living. No one never told us that we could not build the world for the world to come here, even if they do, we do not let their opinions and expertise determine our destiny. We were meant to be a shining beacon of light and inspiration not because it is easy but because we can and for God's glory to be seen in our rags to riches story.

Do you remember the saying that goes *"the hand that gives is the hand that rules"* and even the scriptures say, *"There is much more happiness in giving than in receiving?"*

Will we ever live to our fullest capacity if we are a nation that always begs and depends on other nations and the Bretton Woods institutions?

Let us not forget what we celebrate on the 18th of April annually which is *independence* and not *in dependence day.* Let this serve as a gentle reminder to all of us that we are a sovereign and free country that needs its space to be whoever that we want to be.

Have we forgotten the saying that each man for himself and God for us all this is a testament that everyone shall be a result of their genius and the generous hand of God?

This also applies to nations that each nation will become master of its affairs and then Divine intervention will turn their blood, sweat and tears into progress, prosperity and wealth for the citizens.

If we continue with this syndrome of ours what difference would we have from a family that waits for its neighbors to come to tell them what to eat, how to cook, how to dress and even seek their permission to go outside and bask the sun?

The dependency syndrome has brought nothing apart from the death of our culture, creativity and ourselves which has resulted in our misery and us being poorer and poorer.

Always remember that we are an independent nation and we were all born with free will therefore whatever our nation shall be it is from our creative genius us the inhabitants.

Zimbabwe shall be built by the creative genius of its people for the best quality of life for its people at home or abroad, the born and the yet unborn.

Short sightedness

There is never a death-trap in a nation living in the 21st century that surpasses being short-sighted. The day and age we are living in require us to be way ahead of time for the world is moving faster than ever before so we need to be strategic and visionary in our planning to account for future losses and disruptions.

The most fragile part when it comes to is that it is a very small and pocket change to some nations on the globe. This should serve as a wakeup call that our economy is someone's net worth.

We are in such a vulnerable state because who knows they might wake up and decide to buy us. What will we do if we do not have the economic muscle to defend ourselves?

To prevent our vulnerability in the future we need to be paranoid enough to have the curiosity and the audacity to see future thirty to sixty years from now.

This is no longer the century of having a five-year economic plan like what the Russians did in the 1920s. See, when Lenin came to power it was long back and it took time to see a new invention and even to get information.

What we are looking for is not just merely a developmental plan or strategy or a modernization one but a transformational one that will make us catch up with the rest of the world.

We are Three Industrial Revolutions behind and a five -year modernization plan is not strategic enough to catch up with the rest of the world. This is a matter of life and death or being behind and beyond we are behind and beyond repair therefore it is better we design something new.

We need to have an eagle's view of how we see the world and the future in particular. Yes, our economies need an immediate solution, but quick fixes will not let us be an economic miracle but an economic myth.

Now is the time to begin planning for the next generation and their children. it is time we start having a forty or even sixty- year outlook of what we intend to do and what we shall do if the sun decides to set on the north and not on the west.

It is like we are going on a journey and we need to prepare for a breakdown along the way so we should be planning our stops, for recesses and even our toll fees along the way.

Right now, it is not an ample time to discuss 2030 we should have envisioned it may be in 1990. Now we should be building the future airplane, future bus, future cities, future houses and networks of 2050 or even 2070.

A five year or ten- year plan is not enough; it is a milestone and not an overall end of the journey. We should start seeing beyond our time for the future belongs to the ones who see it first.

Technology giants like Apple and Microsoft rose at the expense of the short-sighted visions of already existing companies like IBM and Xerox. I pray that we too rise from the short-sightedness of other nations and not the other way round.

We should not be like monkeys who when presented with a million dollars and bananas will choose bananas for, they do not know the power of a million dollars that it can buy them many bananas or even a plantation of bananas that can produce more and more bananas for generations to come.

We are faced with the same dilemma that we want quick fixes to feed our mouths and stomachs for today and forgetting how we can be sustainable enough to keep on putting food on the table without hustle. Not all that is presented in front of our eyes is the best like the statement that goes *"not all that glitters are gold"*.

Let us not be deceived by the small loans, grants and foreign direct investment for they do not mean that we automatically have a bright and secure future or the best quality of life.

All these things have been present in Africa ever since Kwame Nkrumah's time and Ghana is still a third world economy around the same time countries like South Korea were built and they created companies like Samsung, Hyundai and Lucky Goldstar and today they are first world countries.

Our neighbor South Africa has attracted massive capital injection but there is little indigenous control and massive inequality makes it one of the unequal countries in the world. This has resulted in social unrest like crime is on the rise and xenophobic attacks have become a trend.

Despite being one of Africa's biggest economies and the most developed countries it is not a haven because of its crime that has resulted more from inequality and poverty amongst the indigenous people.

These are just examples of those close to home, but examples are countless. We are not saying grants and FDI are bad, but they should also cater to the people at home's social well-being.

Also, before we give foreigners access to our industries, we should be able to identify whether we have people who are in the same business and given experience and they should be given first preference.

If the deals do not contribute to the wellbeing of our people, they should be nullified before they are even signed. We are not saying foreigners should not come to our country, but they should invest according to our terms and they can even partner with the Zimbabweans already in business.

Short-sighted visions have become our downfall as African countries and generational planning is also a missing ingredient in the making of our visions. We tend to ignore other stakeholders which are the future generations in our planning and forgetting that one day when we are all gone, they will be the ones inhabiting this country so we cannot afford to live a legacy of poverty.

Poverty is also another key element that usually results from living in dependence and we cannot continue being a nation that depends on the benevolence of other nations forever and ever. If it means, we are to wear glasses in our country to fix our sight then we ought to for the sake of the opportunities that are presented in front of us.

Zimbabwe has got a lot of potentials that remains untapped. We cannot afford to waste our potential by seeing things as they are and not what they could be. If we are to focus more on the future than fixing the present, we will subconsciously fix what bothers us today and pave the way for a new reality that is free of the problems we have today.

Let us not deny ourselves the opportunities that lie ahead of us by blindfolding ourselves but instead let us open our eyes and see the opportunities that lie ahead of us.

The future is quite rewarding for those with the audacity and bravery to face it boldly without hesitation and those who do not shy away from it. The future possibilities should not be limited by the present realities of what is happening today.

Our destination is what matters the most, the journey might be bumpy and rough, but it does not mean that we will not get there, the roughness of the journey does not change the destination.

Therefore, my fellow brothers and sisters the farther we see the further we shall reach as a nation. We are never taxed or arrested for seeing farther but we are rewarded for that

Polarization

This has brought nothing except for divisions, negative energy and a cold war amongst the majority of the citizens and even in our institutions.

Polarization has resulted in the citizens thinking that politics is a war you should pick a side, and this has resulted in the majority being divided into two main camps which are the governing party and the opposition party.

Now, because of these two main camps it's a tug of war of who has got the ear of the masses, who is popular, and they just end up opposing each other for the sake of opposing one another now the country is full of negative energy.

Tensions are high and our country is in a Cold war but this time it is not the East versus the West but it is Right Vs Left, it is a family feud this time whereby the family cannot let go of their ego and reunite.

This is a dispute between the parents forcing the children to choose a side and they are convinced that they cannot find a way to make both parents co-exist. This is a war of power and significance with absolutely nothing to do with the people and the greater good of the country.

We are building a wall against each other, promoting barriers to see who will lose and surrender by tearing their wall down. Instead we should be building bridges for one another and not erecting walls to avoid one another.

Now both camps do whatever they can to sabotage one another to create an impact and shake their opponents.

We cannot afford living like this we are getting old and the clock is ticking we cannot afford to continue playing hide and seek as a nation whilst other nations are moving. Both sides seem to see no fault on their part it is always the fault of the other side, they both have the childhood *"it's not my fault"* type of attitude.

They both manipulate and influence their way out by any means necessary so that they appear clean and better than the other to gain more followers. This is another deceiving old friend we ought to bid farewell to at this moment and for good.

We cannot run a nation like a battlefield whereby when we look at our society, we see enemies and our men but instead it should be a social enterprise whereby we see stakeholders from our communities.

The job is not to segment people due to their differences but to reconcile those differences and make them co-exist and support one other. We have become contained by unnecessary battles but forgetting the "actual war" that lies ahead of us which is transforming our country.

We are forgetting that we are closing doors and opportunities on ourselves to sustain other individuals in power but we are murdering our future and our children's future in doing so.

We can go another forty years in the same state with the one we in today with such processes. After all, has been said and done Zimbabwe needs to push and pull in one direction, but the power mongers have divided us. We are being robbed of our future and destiny by old processes that do not work for us.

The Next Generation vs The Next General Election

The Ugandan opposition leader Bobbi Wine once said that *"the African leaders seem not to care about the next generation but the next general election"*. This is a strategy that has failed us for a very long time and up to date, which is banking our future and children's future on elections.

We have to understand that elections are a means to an end, not the end itself and there are many means other means we can use to get to the end. Right now, we are all stuck on the paradigm that through changing a leader or engaging in elections we automatically wipe away our problems.

Even if our political parties have got the intention of building a strong country, they are overshadowed by one big idea which is to seek the election victory first then everything else will follow.

They fail to see that the biggest visionary mandate that one has to possess is the drive, ability and capacity to advance the social well-being of the people to that of a higher economic state.

Even if it is not election time both parties are always looking for ways in which they could retain or attain power in the next election. It is quite the norm to find that we have got candidates for office in the next 5 years, but we do not have basic goods for next week like fuel and bread or even the faith that we will survive tomorrow.

Our future and present are at stake but for how long and at whose expense shall we keep on being prisoners of hope waiting for the next general election? Right now, other nations are planning that when a newly born baby gets 18, they will have maybe 10G network and we are at rallies chanting empty slogans.

We are disadvantaging the next generation for what wealth will leave behind for them. Party regalia?

Even if the elections are free and fair what if a demagogue who is clueless in running the country manipulates people into electing them? Do we wait for the next general election?

How will we be running our country and living all along? Who says power is being in office alone to my understanding; power is the ability to change the existing reality into a new one?

Even the fathers of philosophy like Socrates where highly pessimistic about the democratic model itself despite it being one of the greatest achievements of their society.

He even argued in Book Six of The Republic that.

"Voting in an election is a skill, not a random intuition. And like any skill, it needs to be taught systematically to people. Letting the citizenry vote without an education is as irresponsible as putting them in charge of a trireme sailing to Samos in a storm".

The model assumes that the electorate is highly knowledgeable about whom they will choose then gives them control and they end up choosing orators and not doctors with the remedy that will heal the pain of the society.

Because of politicking and populist politics the electorate will end up having the wrong people in the office because they are seeking easy answers, or they are told what they want to hear and then their hearts are stolen.

I believe that what matters isn't really who the captain is, but are we following our designated route to get to the end. The end is still that vision we all carry to bed and wake up in pursuit of every day which is having a prosperous and great Zimbabwe in our time and in all time.

It does not mean that if the opposition is not in the office, they cannot change things. Now, every politician's end is the political office and even when they get into office, they have no other vision apart from seeking office again because that is the only vision they carry.

That is why we have politicians in Africa fighting for power when they get into office they fail and then seek another term in office, the process repeats itself till they overstay in power and people get fed up with them.

It because Politicians spend the first half of their political career seeking office and then the second half of their political career consolidating and sustaining the power without changing anything.

Usually, their end is different from ours, but they coerce us into following their end, by convincing us that without them being in office nothing will happen then we all look forward to the next election like it is *"Christ's second coming"*.

But the plight continues even after the elections so why should we continue using the same model?

Other nations are racing towards making electric cars, colonizing Mars and who knows maybe planning for the next revolution after the Fourth Industrial Revolution and we are doing what? We are racing towards a ballot, rallies, demos, and marches that usually result in deaths of many innocent people becoming statistics and forgotten along the way.

That will always be our routine till the next election, and we are told that this time our victory is certain. I appreciate all these efforts that our leaders have done but it's time we go back to the drawing board and draw another game plan because this one is not working.

What if we approached our struggle from a social cause and with the knowledge and wisdom that we all can't be in office? What we need urgently are industries, jobs, money and the best quality of life and above all to be counted on amongst the other nations.

None of all the things mentioned above are built at rallies or demos or during an election but by harnessing our divine power, mastering our creativity and fostering a spirit of enterprise in our people.

I strongly believe that we need to create a transformational plan that will leap-frog us into the future and make us catch up with the rest of the world in a short time. This is not rocket science it has been done before by other countries like Singapore, China, Western Europe amongst others.

If only the right strategies are implemented Zimbabwe can be an economic miracle and we can see it move from Third World to First World within a very short space of time. The choice is ours it's either we sacrifice for the next general election at the expense of the next generation or it is the other way round.

Undervaluing Ourselves

We are turning ourselves into a nation of beggars and falling for anything that comes along our way for we have become so desperate to be part of the *"International Community"*.

Our leaders are always en route to other continents for approval, to convince other nations that they are more important than us and they have a role to play in our nation's prosperity.

We are a nation that is rich and blessed with resources that amount to trillions of dollars I believe. Apart from natural resources we have got many people with ideas that can also amount to trillions of dollars.

Truth be told we are not just irresistible enough to attract the resources that we need to transform and modernize our economy.

We do not need to fly across the Pacific or Atlantic to convince people that we are *"open for business"* or having people protesting in the streets of New York to convince the world that we are open for business.

If we are, we just attract them or meet them along our way. Imagine if you are going to Mutare, do you have to go all over Zimbabwe looking for people to embark on the journey with you?

To save time and resources all you have to do is to start going to Mutare then along the way you will meet people going there and they will join you.

Don't we all think it is a little bizarre and weird when a pretty girl goes everywhere looking for suitors telling every male she meets along the way that she is ready for marriage?

Zimbabwe has got the potential to become the most sought-after girl in the African neighborhood that every man can't get his eyes off, but she isn't just packaged enough to be such a magnet.

Her parents are undervaluing her they don't see the power she has, they are grooming her to be naïve, to settle for less *(Kufira Mafufu Segonzo)* and settling for any man that comes her way.

Her parents are failing to see her intellectual wealth which is intangible that she is not just an ordinary girl but a girl with degrees, exposure, ambitions of her own of being amongst the best in the world; all they think is that she should just get married and start a family.

This is what our leaders are doing; traveling around the world looking for strategic partnerships and come back with promises which do not even materialize. It is because we haven't sold the *Zimbabwean Dream* yet to the world of our intellectual capital that is worth trillions of dollars.

Instead, we go there as beggars asking for pocket change and we expect it to change our country tremendously. They go there "humble" themselves then ask for breadcrumbs instead of the bread at the table and expect to make a sandwich from breadcrumbs and finish our hunger. They label us poor to get more aid and the *"generous hand"* of the *"rich nation"* that do not work it has never worked and it will not work.

It is high time we begin selling the value and selling what we can be in the future. We are a very great brand, but we need great salesmen to sell our brand to our global customers, we should stop using our media to promote negative messages or images of our country but instead positive images. Whenever we paint a positive image of our country, we begin selling a positive brand for our country.

What makes America, Dubai, Singapore and even our fellow brother Rwanda a dreamland for most people is the branding that makes us love them. We should start selling the invisible to the world that Zimbabwe is the prettiest girl in Africa who can win a beauty pageant and become Miss Africa.

We can be Africa's number one economy in the next generation, and we should start walking in that space to attract what we need no one knows our value except for us. With all the trillions we have in our reserves it is not realistic to say that Zimbabwe is still one of the most broke nations on earth. How, can a beautiful girl fail to find suitors or even admirers?

Is it a problem that requires her to be cleansed spiritually? Or, it's just that she has failed to know her worth or she wasn't just packaged enough where she came from? From my understanding I believe that Zimbabwe is one of the few nations that hold the keys to the doors of African Transformation. Therefore, I believe that our progress here in Zimbabwe shall also be a benchmark of progress for other African nations basically the *Zimbabwean dream* will be exported beyond our borders as the *African dream.*

It shall all start in Zimbabwe and end in other African nations for they say *"Charity begins at home and does not end there"* we shall start by giving a real taste of transformation to our Zimbabwean brothers but also not forgetting our future 2.4 billion in our African community.

We are going to be the place where things will be happening in Africa and the long run in the world because the future is Pan African and also Zimbabwean shall be the epicenter of African growth.

My dream, hope, and wish is to see us painting a picture of what Zimbabwe could be to the world and not really what it is. I believe this is not its state but rather a temporary state for nothing lasts forever.

It is time for you and me to sell and export our greatest treasure and mineral Our Zimbabwean Dream to the world and stop undervaluing ourselves but rather convincing our consumers the benefits of buying into the future Zimbabwe amongst the endless possibilities of being part of this future historical moment that are we about to create.

Debt fixing strategies

I believe that this shouldn't be the main strategic imperative for our nation right now for it is not a transformational tool but rather a transactional one. This leaves the national coffers broke with no income to pay for the existing loans or even money to revitalize the existing industries and also to create new ones.

Henceforth, we are left with no option but rather to sell our public companies to the foreign nations and then create a foreign-controlled economy by giving them unconditional rights then they begin controlling our wealth. All we get in the long run are jobs maybe just menial ones and the managerial ones are left for foreigners and the guise of "experience".

We end up earning peanuts and will never even tackle poverty and transform our communities. It is because the paradigm itself is just a transactional one and also does not give us any momentum.

The mistake here is that the IMF was never designed to transform economies but instead to be monitors who were preventing another Great Depression, reducing debt and balance of payments so they were never designed to be engineers but technical people who maintain the order as it is.

But where would a country get the capital from to finance its projects if it does not borrow and how will it run or even modernize? The IMF strategies aren't entrepreneurial but more of technical money math strategies and they make them look like modern-day Third World tax collectors who rob us of our wealth with briefcases.

Said Elias Dawlabani the author of Memenomics: The Next Generation Economics says that *"Money is to an economy as nutrition is to the human body. When central banks ignore the relationship by providing more capital that is functionally needed, they debase everything that capitalism stands for".*

Isn't their model (IMF) destroying our enterprise, how are we going to modernize our economy when it is malnourished with no adequate budgets? This system will never give us any momentum in the future. Debt fixing will never get Zimbabwe into the promised land our predestined land of honey and milk. It is keeping us in the desert without rivers of wealth flowing but instead burning from the scorching heat of poverty and misery.

The Bretton Woods institutions use a demand management system that simply translates to "payback or you shall see" and has created panic strategies in many African countries including Zimbabwe as well. Have we forgotten, the Economic Structural Adjustment Program

(ESAP) in Zimbabwe that uncivilized our people, devalued our currencies and created a financial crisis in Zimbabwe? Have we been able to bounce back ever since the ESAP period?

Statistics do not only speak for themselves but also the events that were to occur after ESAP. The main objectives of the program were never achieved, and it was just a failed technical strategy that was never fit for our country.

For example, if you look at some of their objectives like.

- achieving a GDP growth of 5% by from 1991-1995
- raising savings to 25% of GDP
- raising investments to 25% of GDP
- reducing the budget deficit from over 10% of GDP to 5% by 1995
- reducing inflation from 17.7% to 10% by 1995.

Most of these objectives failed and led our country down to the drain. I believe that is where the mess started, and I am convinced we still haven't found our way out.

If you were to look at the events that transpired after 1995 that is when you see our graph falling and never rising again. Despite the statistical results showing us the failure, they were also events like the 1997 strikes which were recorded to be over two hundred in one year alone because of the retrenchment of workers and low salaries. There was also the 14 November stock market crash in 1998 because the economy was ailing, and companies were struggling to remain profitable in such an environment.

Moving on to the statistical results the effects were very disastrous for example:

• economic growth decelerated from an average of 4% before ESAP to 1,4%   during the ESAP period

• inflation rose by an average of 27.6% compared to 11.6% before ESAP

• deterioration of the budget deficit from 10% of GDP to 12.2% by 1995.

• Higher levels of poverty in rural areas (75%)

• An increase in the incidence of poverty from 16.7% to 35.7% amongst many other factors.

NB: All the statistical information on this topic was adapted from the data compiled by the Central Statistical Office (1998), Poverty Assessment Study Survey of the Ministry of Public Services, and Social Welfare Zimbabwe (1995).

Now this is the history which they say repeats itself and I believe that it does so when we do not take action or when we do not take lessons from the events of the past. These are all cues and clues that the Universe gives us not to fall into the trap of the Bretton Woods institutions that keep us regressing.

We can even take a look at the present day *"Austerity to Prosperity"* path in Zimbabwe which has seen hyperinflation, protests, the rise of parallel markets controlling the finance of the country. So, why are we continuing with the same processes? We should do away with the folly that the IMF is empathetic towards us and that they will lift us of misery and make us catch up with the rest of the world.

Since its founding and the independence of African nations we haven't seen any transformational ideas coming from the IMF except for Structural Adjustment Programmes in our economies that usually devalued our currencies and cutting our budgets. Zimbabwe will need its Modernization budget that is adequate and fit for it to drive its transformation for the number one priority right now is economic transformation and debt management is just an objective.

More capital in our economy is like more oxygen and blood for us to live and so is something that should be in abundant supply if we want to live healthily. As far as I am concerned with debt management it is like our economy is on life support and finding it hard to breathe on its own for the economic oxygen *(capital)* is in short supply.

Every economic miracle that we hear of or admire came from a disastrous financial state that could have been worse than Zimbabwe. They knew the strategic imperative during that time was transforming their economies so that they wouldn't remain in the same state forever.

It would never have been a miracle if they were no disasters before, China, Japan, Singapore and South Korea were once amongst the most broke nations financially, but they transformed without Bretton Woods institutions therefore, why can't we do the same?

Are these countries philosophically superior to us? No, I do not believe that, the problem is that we are just chasing skunks and whatever comes in our way. We forget that we do not eat skunks and our other mates spend the day chasing after what is edible.

At the end of the day we go to them asking for the same meat that we ignored in the jungle whilst we were chasing after skunks. Isn't it very absurd and ingenious?

Capital, capital, capital is what we need to leapfrog our economy and prioritizing debt management is an impediment and an enemy of our economic transformation. I believe for one to become an expert it is a matter of experience that makes one an expert. I believe when it comes to designing the future, we have no expert because no one knows what it looks like no one has ever been there.

The problem with experts is that because they are used to their old paradigms, they end up convincing us that there is no other way to drive our nation forward except the one they chart for us.

They never tell us we can, they always think of what it is and not what it can be, they are like prophets of doom which never see the impossible becoming inevitable but instead the inevitable becoming impossible.

As they say if you cannot simplify it you cannot solve it the experts have not yet simplified our problems by creating one simple leading idea and what to do to achieve success in our nation.

Yes, our problems are complex but not complicated they become complicated when we operate at a technocratic level and not as men and women we were born to be. John Fitzgerald Kennedy once said that *"all our problems are manmade and therefore no problem is beyond human destiny"*, hence this means we can solve the Zimbabwean problems organically.

Why do they hurry to criticize and advise us on our national visions telling us that we are engaging in wishful thinking and that we will not make it? Let us not be blindfolded by technical expertise for history teaches us that they were many other nations who came from a far more disadvantaged position than ours, but it took bravery from transformational leaders to shame the dark spells that had been cast on them by these experts.

We all know what happened to Japan after World War 2 and its global ascension within a short space of time because of General Saito. What about the state in which Singapore was in after its independence and separation from Malaysia? Now imagine what it became after Lee Kuan Yew took it in another radical transformational direction.

South Korea had devastating results after the Korean War and was one of the poorest nations in the world with a per capita below US$100 but Park Chung-hee created a new course for the nation with a simple leading idea and concept of intent.

Today we all know them because of big chaebols like Samsung, Hyundai and LG. The world never saw it coming but today it is a reality. Which expert saw Apple, Microsoft, even Coca-Cola coming?

I guess it was just a matter of innovation and invention that these things were discovered along the way after they were imagined hence it needed no expert to tell them to do so. Experts are born out of experience hitherto, there was no moon landing expert before the first man landed on the moon but as they started going there continuously, the experience was built, and they became experts in the long run.

I believe it is time we ignore the noise and start RETHINKING Zimbabwe without putting expertise in the front but instead as how we were born. It all takes a simple leading idea to drive us into the future, but experts never give us one simple leading idea into the future. All they have done is giving us complicated fancy terms that we will never feast on and it is like explaining the digestive system of an ant to a farmer.

The golden question here is if experts see the future than everyone else why couldn't they see the major global financial crises like in 2008? Besides the 2008 one why didn't they learn after the crises that occurred before like the 1997 Asian and 1998 Russian crises to prevent 2008 from happening?

Well, because most of them operate on a technical level and the few who operate organically are overshadowed by the majority in the technical space. They are operating as jobbers not as futurists they just do what matches their job description.

In conclusion the future is invented by those with an intuitive foresight, those who possess an eagle's view, those who believe in the endless possibilities of the future and ultimately those who are inspired by the future picture and not what the present.

Creating New Value

More than anything else, Zimbabwe needs a new idea that creates value for the future. We must begin to move with the idea that *"We hold the keys to African transformation and solving Zimbabwe is solving Africa"*. If we take long, we are delaying our fellow African brothers and sisters towards progression.

Zimbabwe is predestined to be the Giant of the African continent, the hub and even the leader in African transformation. When Robert Mugabe inherited this land during Independence Mwalimu Julius Nyerere is believed to have told him that *"You have inherited the jewel of Africa"* and I was told by a fellow Ghanaian that *"Nothing will change in Africa until something changes in Zimbabwe".*

Could this be a coincidence that two different generations of Africans which are the liberators and the born free coming from the Eastern and the Western parts of Africa all said the same thing about one nation?

Well I tried to go back to my history books, and I looked at both modern-day history and ancient history. Starting with ancient history, it is believed that King Solomon's Ophir was positioned in Zimbabwe now, just imagine the amount of strategic importance that Zimbabwe had in Africa and the world.

What about when Great Zimbabwe was built, how many traders passed through it? How important was it to the economy of its region and beyond? In the 1950s when we were still a colony during the federation of Rhodesia and Nyasaland the industries and the administration was down here in Southern Rhodesia (Zimbabwe). If you read in between the lines it is not just a coincidence but rather historical signals to prove that this nation has to lead in the process of African economic transformation.

The choice is ours either to be predators or to be the prey I cannot read minds but for one time I can guess that in our minds we all choose to be the former. I wish that every Zimbabwean would go about with the gospel that *"The Road to African prosperity passes through their doorstep"*.

The Cradle of African Innovation

Zimbabwe has always been of strategic importance to Africa and the world for a very long time both in ancient and modern-day history. It is believed that King Solomon's Ophir was located in present-day Zimbabwe and this means that Zimbabwe had not only a strategic position in Africa alone but also in the world.

When we look at Great Zimbabwe it was a regional hub for trade also which means it had an economic impact on the region and beyond. During colonial times when the Federation of Rhodesia and Nyasaland was formed in 1954, Zimbabwe was where things were happening, and many migrated from Malawi and Zambia in search of greener pastures.

Let us not forget that it wasn't until yesteryear when Zimbabwe was called the Breadbasket of Africa because we fed the world. Even during independence Julius Mwalimu Nyerere told Mugabe that he was inheriting the Jewel of

Africa. I was once told by a Ghanaian friend that *"Nothing will change in Africa until something happens in Zimbabwe"*.

Is this a coincidence or a historical mistake? No, I believe we have the calling to be the African Giant all these were just steppingstones for us to get to our predestined land of honey and milk.

The imperative now is to position ourselves as Africa's Industrial Basket where Industrialization and Modernization shall happen. We are going to build the hubs here in Zimbabwe and catch up with the world very soon if only we do the right thing.

We are going to move major industries and build ours here in Zimbabwe and turn Zimbabwe into the most industrialized nation in Africa per square foot if it needs to be. We can be the first African country to manufacture airplanes, rail stock and even create one of the biggest hubs for the 4IR (the Fourth Industrial Revolution) in the world. We shall be the next Munich, Silicon Valley and Tsinghua all in one where innovators and industrial leaders come from.

This has never happened in Africa and it is a chance for Zimbabwe to lead by example and get known by the world for the right reasons. Imagine how much wealth we are going to create for ourselves, our children and for the next generations.

South Korea made much wealth from manufacturing semiconductors and electronics. What about if we manufacture almost anything from small components to trains and airplanes?

Africa is the place where things will be happening why don't we position ourselves for that as a nation. We are going to add more value to anything that we used to export and export it when processed.

Why do we import medicine at exorbitant prices when we have herbs all over our country and people who have studied and still study pharmacy? What stops us from building as a pharmaceutical hub for Africa and the world at large?

In everything that we shall be in the future it does not matter how much population we have we can attract the geniuses from Africa and the world. It is what we bring to the table that matters meaning if we need to be a great global player and partner, we should start positioning ourselves here as an African Giant.

South Korea, Singapore, China were merely just ghosted nations that had no strategic importance to the world, but we saw miracles happening from them. China transformed within a space of twenty-five years and now challenging the USA for the top spot.

South Korea is now amongst the G-20 nations and has produced big brands like Samsung, LG and Hyundai.

Singapore has moved from being third to the first world in one generation and was far worse than the present situation in Zimbabwe today.

Who knew that one day the world would be flying jetliners made in Central America particularly in Brazil? They never saw it coming and they will never see us coming but we are coming for them. It shall be a miracle and a story taught for generations to come we cross the Red Sea from poverty to riches.

We are in a better position than many nations that did it before us because we have a lot to learn from them and also, they are new technologies that will enable us to do the task faster.

What took Singapore 40 years should not take us the same but instead take us 25 years' maximum that is if we are fail which is not happening on my watch. I tell you that in one generation Zimbabwe can move from its disastrous state to a prosperous state that will leave the world in a state of shock. Just because we have fertile lands does not mean we have to rely solely on agriculture or mining.

We ought to diversify in case that year we have a drought or prices for raw materials fluctuate. They say you do not put all your eggs in one basket and the American industrialist Andrew Carnegie is believed to have said that *"Put all your eggs in one basket and watch them"* to Africa I say put all industries industrial basket (Zimbabwe) and watch them thrive.

Made in Zimbabwe

Apart from bringing the big players into Zimbabwe like the Fortune 500, we should also begin our process of creating Zimbabwe's big brands. Imagine all the thinkers that we have, the entrepreneurs and visionaries in our youths.

Imagine what the future would look if we supported them and promote such a spirit amongst our young men and women. It is time we begin exporting our goods and brands to the world. I have a dream that one day we shall sell manufactured automobiles, clothes, gadgets and even toothbrushes to the world at large. I have a dream that one day one of our Zimbabwean companies will be a partner at a global event like the Football World Cup comparable to what Coca- Cola does. What stops a Zimbabwean brand like Dairiboard to be like that?

A time shall come when we shall build Zimbabwe that our children will not leave Zimbabwe and go into the world but instead the world will come to us. Maybe, someday Siyaso and Magaba would be manufacturing goods that will be exported globally because already they are rivals to big well-established industries imagine if they have adequate funding and well-advanced machinery.

It might sound insane or too farfetched or like a false prophecy, but it is achievable so long as we envision it ourselves that way, we can achieve it. Who thought that after Hiroshima and Nagasaki Japan would rival the USA in the automobile industry amidst the fact that the USA had big brands like General Motors, Ford etc.? Who thought that Japanese cameras would replace German cameras like Zeiss? Well no one saw it coming for no one can read minds or stop an idea whose time to manifest has come.

We have the natural resources and what is left is aligning them with our human resources so that we see material benefits. We have got Zimbabweans who are doing phenomenal things all across the world and who wouldn't be hurt to do something for their country for example we have an architectural firm called "Vavaki" based in the United Kingdom that designed the Kigali Heights one of Rwanda's most modern buildings.

We have William Pasi Sachiti who created an autonomous vehicle in the United Kingdom as well. We have a young man who built his electric car here in Zimbabwe so can we not make money from this? One-day people in America will have to drive Zimbabwean cars on the roads of New York, Washington, Chicago and even Texas.

The same way we rush into Japanese, Chinese, Portuguese, Greek restaurants shall be the same way the world will race to Zimbabwean restaurants enjoying our *"sadza, madora, mutsine, nyevhe"*, etc.

Come to think of its pizza is Italy's staple food like sadza is to us but here in Zimbabwe, it is expensive because it is exotic. What about sushi is it expensive in Japan as it is here in Zimbabwe? Why can't our "*mutakura, mahewu*" be sold in Japan and New York?

We should be aggressive enough to knock on the doorstep of the world and sell our products that are originally from Zimbabwe. Our designers should be on stage in Italy, France, London fashion weeks with celebrities wearing clothes made in Zimbabwe.

All I can say is we already have the necessary tools to build Global Empires, but we are in dire need of salesman to sell the brand. From what we have, our creative minds and our capital we shall build a strong Zimbabwean economy. Which is what I would love to call the *Made in Zimbabwe* concept machine.

Time to study the greats till we become the greatest

We need to understand where we are and where we want to be in the near future for if we do not desire to be some -where we will be nowhere and anywhere one of these fine days.

Right now, we are in a state of destitution, turmoil and a disastrous state. We all want to be rescued from the ruins of the demolished structure first because we are in dire need of assistance.

We are languishing in the prison of misery and poverty. We are all tired of it and we are looking for parole or an escape plan. Now we need to go into the Global neighborhood and see what sort of houses are being built and the one we need to build.

We can look at the best in terms of everything from finance, ethics, industry, human development, then I assure you if we master and implement those principles then we shall never be the same again. We shall move from being passengers on the journey of African transformation but instead become the drivers of it and steer the wheel to our own direction.

If you want to be a music legend you will have to study the legends and not the amateurs, so basically what we have to do is to see globally and implement locally. It is a race against the world and not just for survival but also a race for significance.

We do not have to re-invent the wheel but to take the wheel that is already there and make it cooler to see what it lacks then add more value to it.

The Pirates of Silicon Valley did not invent computers, but they just added cooler components and created value for themselves. Japan did not invent cars, but they worked on the already existing models, created smaller, affordable ones and sold them to the world making wealth in the long run.

The beauty of benchmarking is that you will always find a loophole and make what is already there, cooler in the name of innovation. Zimbabwe can find, learn from the best and then decide whether they want to be like them or better then start progressing towards the objective.

Let us accept that we are already behind we need to catch up with the world and it requires us to act fast enough because the world is not waiting. There are many nations we can learn from and all we have to do is to see what applies in our day to day lives.

We can copy and paste principles and even models so long as they suit our realities for universal principles are principles, they see no race, nor the religion and even location. The path is clear and all we have to do is decide when we start moving this is not the time to think but it is time to do. We are in destitution; we are in a jungle full of predators and we need to move faster than we can to get to safe territory.

Unfortunately, because of who gets there first and finder takes all rules of Capitalism there is nowhere safe we need to keep on running and to never relax for the predators strike unexpectedly meaning we need to be prepared to fight back. Once we see the gaps in whomever we learn from then we can just beat them in their own game by changing the rules of the game slightly but on the same playing field and the game becomes completely a new one.

Like what the Americans did to rugby by creating American football, from cricket to baseball. Even the creation of checkers after chess with checkers having different rules but being played on a chessboard. All these people either knew they would never win games they did not create for they were not designed in their favor and all games are won by f so they decided to make their games from their own rules.

We will never beat our competitors at their own game unless we find a loophole then create our games from their games by inviting them to the contest and then become the winners. If we do not understand the rules of the game that we are playing, we will never be masters of that game and we can never be masters of something that we never created.

We are going to go into the world and learn their systems and model them to our advantage and innovate the new from there. By the time we implement this concept whoever where the leaders will be fighting for a second place simply because they had a false start. We will capitalize on their weaknesses and turn them into our point of strength and advantage. So just open your eyes woooh!

Whenever we see a world crisis soon or a flaw in any system it is our opportunity to manifest greatness for like I said before; our nation has a divine anointing to lead African transformation and this century shall see the rise of Africa and we shall lead it. All our students, professionals and even ordinary citizens who are all over the world will make Zimbabwe transform itself, why? Because we are going to package all they have learned into one simple leading idea that will give us a landslide victory over our other competitors because of the exposure that we have.

Our time is now, we can always start today, we have nothing to lose for we have already lost, and we cannot reverse the calendar but instead we can change the ending of our story.

Along the process we have much to gain because we have a lot ahead of us. What we need is a **GLOCAL** approach to our everyday way of life, we need to see things from a global approach and implement what is applicable locally. It is time to do away with the peasant worldview and not confining ourselves to the tuck shop mentality that is how we build a Global Empire.

We should move with the psychology that whatever we do has Global effects and we should always compare what we do with the standards of the world and if we do not match Global standards then we stop doing whatever we are doing. Let us not confine ourselves to the small mindset and mentality for the world is ours too we are also stakeholders of the Global markets too so we should behave as such.

Recreate Zimbabwe Vision

After we crush old processes it is crucial that we create a new vision for our country that is quite powerful and motivational. Not everyone will rally behind it, but it will have the majority rallying behind it, but it should be an idea powerful enough to encourage the citizenry to rise up against all odds and fulfill their inner quests in a way that will benefit society.

After we see what the world is like and its environmental behavioral patterns, we need to craft a new vision from the current world views. After the process of benchmarking we already know what we want to do and whom we want to surpass.

A new consciousness is born creating the need for change therefore a new vision for a nation is needed urgently. The state of mind that is floating in Zimbabwe by that time will be of prosperity and global competitiveness, so we are thinking big and starting small.

When an idea begins manifesting it becomes something that floats all over and it creates a critical mass it becomes part of people's second nature apart from just breathing.

The idea then becomes part of our DNA it is then a natural part of us; that is the power of an idea coming to life it manifests itself the mindset will be endowed with special powers like what Hannington Mubaiwa says.

Having a powerful vision doesn't mean we are going to be 100% perfect nor corruption-free, but it just means we become ethical and focus more on that vision. We are like a child in high school, almost everyone is mischievous, but they are those who pass and make it and they the ones who fail dismally!

Why is it so? Because others have a vision of what they want to be so whatever they do they control themselves and focus on the vision more.

The latter have no vision and are just waking up to anything so they can also do anything, and they do not see future repercussions because they see no future. If we see the future, we cannot afford to sacrifice it to corruption which will give us a new vision that accounts for ethics.

Corruption can be transparent and controlled then if the vision is powerful enough everyone else feels as if they part of a big something like a big movement then we all will be disciplined and ethical enough to achieve what we want. Imagine the day when Zimbabweans marched to remove Mugabe everyone went into the streets jovial, inspired, united and above all disciplined we did not hear any cases of theft, or violence. Everyone was inspired and focused on the future for they had painted a picture of the future which they felt they were going to be part of.

It is like they were having a party and they were all invited so nothing else mattered apart from the future they had painted. All their energy was centered on saying goodbye to the man whom they felt had robbed them of their future and waiting on what tomorrow might bring. In the dream of every Zimbabwean's imagination they were a picture of a better tomorrow that everyone else could follow.

That is what we need right now to sing *"We are marching over to The Promised Land"* united and happy if we could have such an idea that could unite us like that, I tell you we would be a reason why the blind might want to see.

Imagine us marching over to a Zimbabwe with a *Trillion Dollar economy* a Zimbabwe which makes good headlines across the world, a Zimbabwe that answers the woes even that of a common man, a Zimbabwe that answers our needs and wants whereby our rights are respected and honored.(*1trillion dollar economy is a figure calculated using the modernization trends of other developed nations-ref :Mubaiwa*)

Imagine Zimbabwe being the first African country to host the Olympic games. Right now, one of the main objectives should be a Recreate and Rebrand Zimbabwe vision and a completely different view from the way we see it.

It is a myth that economists are the ones that create masterplans or imagine the future of a country's economy but instead it is the citizens who do that by creating a simple leading idea that creates value which unleashes an economic power and identity.

I have stressed and stressed that all we need is a simple leading idea of what Zimbabwe can be and the idea is *"Zimbabwe a Trillion-dollar economy in the next generation and an epicenter for African socio-economic transformation.*

Being an epicenter for African transformation is not the end goal but it is our biggest and faster means for us to cater to the aspirations, needs and goals of our community. We want to be an inspiration to other African countries not to rule them but to take the initiative, we want to get to the mountaintop not for the world to see us but instead to see the world.

After reaching the mountaintop we want to go back into the valley and get our fellow African brothers out of the mud and instead go together to the mountaintop.

Whoever gets there first calls the shots that are the rule of every civilization, so if we can make our path and leave a trail, we can patent the game of African transformation and have the *intellectual property rights* of the 2.4 to 3 billion consumption power in the next generation. I believe whoever solves Zimbabwe solves Africa and the road to *Real African transformation* passes through Zimbabwe. It is not arrogance but rather a conviction that will give us the purpose and zeal to continue when we feel like giving up. It is a reminder that the race for African

Transformation is one we cannot afford to lose in our lifetime.

Our nation should be run like a business but with the purest intent of creating and distributing wealth to the people and then reinvesting the surpluses for future generations that is an idea I have learnt from my mentor Mr. Hannington Mubaiwa and it has made a lot of sense to me. The new imperative for the government should be more of organizing the business of social enterprise versus the ruling and running the country by then. For let us not forget that our vision is an embodiment of our ideas, culture, philosophies, aspirations and economic needs as a nation and in everything we do we all aspire to be prosperous and the government is a strategic organization to focus on Zimbabwean prosperity and not government and politics.

We should all be waking up to an idea from the Zambezi to Limpopo, from the leafy suburbs and expensive estates of Glen Lorne, Borrowdale to the remotest of places like Binga and Uzumba, waking to the idea of prosperity. The duty belongs to the citizenry and the fate of transformation is in their hands. All the central government has to do is to support their capacity for economic activity do as to meet their needs and wants.

Remember that most of the great innovations or life-changing ideas never really came from the government but were a result of the free-thinking of citizens and the ability of their governments to support them. Being free is not just participating in the ballot, but also having a free will and free thinking amongst the citizens which is supported by the structures of that society.

Revelations, epiphanies, and serendipity or even problem-solving ideas created Industrial Revolutions, and all these came from free citizens and the government supported their rich findings making them a citizenry-government partnership in the business of their national enterprise. Queen Isabella didn't download the map of America into Christopher Columbus' head but instead he discovered it on his way to India by serendipity. Neither did the American government give a direct order to Thomas Watson to start IBM.

Did the Japanese government give an order to Konusike Matsushita the order to create Panasonic? Did the Federal Government give Colonel Sanders the recipe for chicken to start KFC or give Ray Kroc the idea to franchise McDonald's? An example that is closer to home did the government give a direct order to Dr. Strive Masiyiwa to start Econet? Even Rhodes wasn't given the order by Queen Victoria to colonize Zimbabwe but instead a Royal Charter to go ahead for they knew it was going to benefit their economy in the long run.

There were a few examples that the governments had to intervene in helping businesses to come up with new ideas for example in South Korea when the government instructed chaebols to explore new business ideas for example when it discouraged Lucky Goldstar (LG) from going into the textile business but instead into the cable business and today LG is one of the biggest and recognized companies in the world. Another example is South Korea when Hyundai was made to go into the ship building business by the government and today it is one of the biggest ship builders in the world. This is an example of a citizenry-government partnership whereby both parties support each other in finding their untapped potential that can create wealth for their national enterprise in a respectable manner.

From all these examples the only duty of the government was to support the rich findings made by their citizens to create wealth for their countries and in the long run it inspired many to follow suit and more innovations and revolutions came. The American government knew that without supporting the Watsons they would have betrayed their vision and whichever citizen came with a spirit of entrepreneurship and a big dream should be supported.

This paved the way for other people like Steve Jobs, Bill Gates, Michael Dell. After them also came to a generation of social network entrepreneurs like Zuckerberg's, Dorsey's, Chen's, Hofmann's, the Brins and Pages only to name a few.

The Japanese knew that without supporting the post Second World War innovations they would be doomed for they were a small island with barely any resources so they had to support their techno-preneurs and it didn't take them much time to bounce back but this time as a leader.

Queen Victoria knew that if she didn't support Cecil John Rhodes on his Cape to Cairo conquest then their long casted vision of conquering the world would have been swindled hence the mantra *The sun never sets on the British Empire* would be a useless one so anyone who came in line with that vision would be supported. By supporting anyone who had a vision in line with their vision by 1914 about 413 million people were part of the British Empire directly and indirectly and that was about a quarter of the earth landmass that was under Britain.

Despite their vision being evil all these people were of strategic importance to them as suppliers and buyers of raw materials. They were the biggest exporters of diamonds without any diamond mining in Britain, and their currency was backed from the gold they had taken from Africa and other countries. It was an idea that was pushed beyond politics that no matter who comes into power either it was the Labor or Conservatives to the rules of the game were the same; *"The sun never sets of the British Empire."* Through that idea Britain became a Global empire and not just economically but spread its English ways and was admired by many nations.

We are creating an empire too but not through colonialism nor guns but market innovation by harnessing the 2.4 to 3 billion consumption power of Africa in the next generation. Just think of it; Britain was the first country to industrialize in the world and with only a sixth of our consumption power can you imagine the endless possibilities here. These years were dubbed as the British centuries. Don't you think this is a Zimbabwean century? That this is our moment that fate has created? A new empire is being born here in Africa but this time not from slave ships nor war but from the creative genius of its people and with the aid of its fellow African brothers.

I don't know about you but I think destiny has given us a glimpse of what tomorrow might look like. I think I have seen the land of honey and milk and I am encouraging you to take a walk with me into the future. We are going to be having twenty-five percent of the world consumers here in Africa closer to home which means no nation can dare to mess with us for *"Zimbabwe holds the keys to African transformation"*. We are just tapping into the untapped, innovating what hasn't been innovated already and positioning ourselves as the *Gentle Lion of Africa*.

The expertise is already there and if the idea becomes bigger than us even then the world would just want to come and experience the Zimbabwean dream helping us in building the brand. This is a promotion that has been presented in front of Zimbabwe not a buy one gets one for free but a *Solve Zimbabwe Solve Africa*. But this has to be done with a sense of urgency for ideas move from a place of higher consciousness to another if we are not fast enough someone will get it and we will continue suffering.

But whatever it is that we do, we should do it peacefully and humbly without invoking war in our continent nor manipulating our brothers and sisters. We just want to be a model for other African nations to emulate and give inspiration that "*where there is a will there is a way*".

We want to show them that Africa can be the master of its fate and that whoever understands the rules of Transformation shall be free from foreign domination and hegemony. Zimbabwe is to be a prototype nation for African transformation as my mentor Hannington Mubaiwa designed in his *"Rapid Africa Plan the Fast Track Modernization of Africa"* that there is a need for a prototype nation. This is an idea that I fell in love with and I believe that it can take Zimbabwe on a new radical path full of endless possibilities.

Our country may seem hopeless now, but the truth is we are an economic miracle in the making, why? Because miracles happen in the least expected of places and the most hopeless places. Imagine if Jesus had woken up a sleeping man who had signs of life compared to raising a dead man would it be a miracle and surprising? No! If Dr. Benjamin Carson had operated a leg of a normal baby would it have made headlines compared to the Siamese twins he operated?

No, again because it would have been normal stories that people hear about every day like someone is dead or a baby is born these things happen every day.

But Zimbabwe seems hopeless that when it rises no one would have anticipated it is going to shock them and then they will get used to it until it becomes normal life to them. We shall create another world wonder and make them eight adding one more to the already seven existing ones, which will be the pace in which our economy can transform and how we will become a Giant in the world.

We shall be a beacon of light and hope, the stars of the human race that they shall us shine as far as outer space if it needs be. Whatever one is destined to be they have it in them already same as Zimbabwe we have all the minds that can change whatever situation we are in and some who are already doing it. Look at Dr. Strive Masiyiwa a man who has built an African telecom business Econet and he is not the only one we also have rising stars who are just waiting for their moment to shine.

We have companies like "Vavaki" that are designing state of the art infrastructure in Africa, imagine one day if they begin to rival companies like Bechtel and other global giants for, we have people with knowledge and global consciousness. Who says that one day the tallest building won't be in Zimbabwe? No one ever said it so why can't it be?

South Korea was way poorer than the North Korean peninsula after the Korean War in the 1950s but today we talk about the Miracle on the Han River and today they are in the G-20 nations. They have moved from an aid receiver to an aid donor this is what we call economic transformation and not growth. One day we will sit at the Global table giving Humanitarian aid to other nations and even having investments both FDI and ODI in as far as Europe, America and Asia adding much wealth in both our local coffers and foreign reserves.

We will have the best social services and that will be free and affordable for everyone. What matters is to have access to every basic human need and want and not mediocre standards but at best they can ever be.

On Corruption

Like I mentioned earlier on our *Zimbabwean dream* shall be exported beyond borders and turn into an *African dream*, our standards are going to be the envy of the rest of the continent this is not an *Alice in Wonderland fantasy* but an idea that shall manifest.

It requires a collective effort both from the citizenry and central government all with a collective attitude towards the dream. We need to be strict on corruption as well and not just by addressing it or targeting political opponents as our sacrificial lambs for corruption accountability. We need contracts that cannot be rubbed off and reversed to prevent it from happening in the first place, then we need stern measures to punish the corrupt.

I believe that this is the greatest nemesis of a vision for it pulls us back. Mind you we are not just stealing from the present coffers but also denying the future generations of their future. Look at the problems we have today they are results of mismanagement that happened previously, and we are where we are because of no accountability and transparency.

Corruption has long term effects that might not be seen presently as we say in our native Shona we say *(Chisi hachiyeri musi wacharimwa)*. It is through corruption that doctors are protesting in the streets and people dying in hospitals. It is through corruption that people queue for money that is not there in banks. It is through corruption that we have no electricity and water and we are in this state of destitution.

Corruption has now become a cancer that is spreading faster than lighting in Zimbabwe, it starts at a high level to the bottom. Here is a relatable example of corruption.

"The school photographer goes to the school head and tells them that photos are going for a dollar each. The school head then goes to the class teacher and tells them that photos

are going for three dollars each. Then the teacher tells their students that photos are going for five dollars each. The student goes home and tells their mother that photos are going for ten dollars. The mother tells the father that there is a photo shoot at school and their child needs fifteen dollars. The Father goes to work and tells his boss that his child is in the hospital they need at least five hundred dollars for settling the medical bills".

That is a corruption for us the cycle goes on and on, if it is not controlled and till the main source is broke. The main source is our national treasury that is now broke and now people queue long hours in front of empty banks waiting for something to happen. This is abnormal, I cannot bear that load and burden I do not want a Zimbabwe like that for myself, children and grandchildren.

This won't take our nation anywhere but instead back to the Stone Age and not into the fourth and fifth Industrial Revolution. How can we fail to have electricity and water in the 21st century and see it as the normal day to day routine? The disorder has now been taken for the normal order and what is normal is now seen as extravagance here in Zimbabwe and all this is because of corruption. If we continue another thirty years like this where will we be? We will be just a failed state and a graveyard because our ways do not go well with our time.

I think there is nothing that is more treasonous than corruption for corruption itself has killed our nation and destroyed it to its foundation that it needs a new foundation of ethics, principles and indelible codes. If we are sixteen million-plus in our population and going to be about forty million in the next thirty years, then everyone swindles a dollar every day how much do we lose daily? We will lose about forty million dollars a day and nearly fifteen billion every year. Imagine the things we could build, create like schools, hospitals, industries or even build houses for our low-income classes. But when that money disappears in thin air it does nothing that benefits the normal citizenry but only a few and the majority do not smell or even taste a dime of that money. Isn't that treason?

Corruption is a moral cancer and the best treatment is a severe punishment to whoever caught stealing from the national coffers to kill it before it spreads across the whole body. We do not want a repetition of the situation we are in because of things we can control and prevent. The other thing is that the vision should be motivational and bigger enough to prevail over corruption. It should be a destination that makes journey and ride worth taking for those who choose to take part in it.

If one becomes corrupt it is a clear testament that they have become enemies of progress and denying change to come to Zimbabwe. Corruption subverts and undermines our inalienable rights. It denies the prosperity of the common people and it even denies their right to be the highest version they were innately created to become.

Besides being against the natural laws and orders of society corruption is also against our African idea of Ubuntu. What has happened to the idea that whatever that I do has got dire consequences for the next person. I believe irrevocable laws and contracts should be created on corruption followed by stern measures and leading by example whoever does that should be brought to justice.

We cannot afford to risk the future and continue suffering because of the things that we can change; this does not even require fasting nor praying but instead acting firmly and strongly on it. Our nation's future is at stake here and we cannot afford to lose our position on the Global table because of corruption and a few individuals whom we can deal with.

Regional Financial Center

Again this an idea that I fell in love with from *"The Rapid Africa Plan: the Fast Track Modernization of Africa"* which was designed by Hannington Mubaiwa which is the idea of the creation of a new financial map for Africa and amongst it was the idea of building regional financial centers in Africa.

His point is The African Union has no macro-economic plan to unite Africa industrially and above all a New Financial Map ever since Kwame Nkrumah's time. In short, Africa has failed to modernize because of the lack of access to capital on the free market. We might want to deny it, but money makes things happen and we need it as a tool of getting whatever we want and need in our day to day lives it is an enabling tool. Mind you there are trillions of dollars on the free market looking for places to go so why can't we be just innovative enough by channeling those funds to ourselves?

If we build a strong industrial base for Africa, I do not see what fails us as a nation to attract more capital inflow into our nation because we are going to grow industrially and they are going to be more innovation and competitiveness and much talent which means the financial institutions would want a taste of the bigger slice of cake.

Another signal we are ignoring is that of the future 3 billion consumption power of Africa by 2050 which they can want to be part of this is an intangible and invaluable resource that Zimbabwe has presented in front of it means all we have to do is to catch up with the future whilst it's still young. If we can sell that benefit to the potential financial partners that we have the keys to about a quarter of the Global markets who would deny that chance.

Another sign is that the African Union has signed the African Continental Free Trade (AfCFTA)Agreement that makes Africa borderless and the question is what they will be trading if we do not produce anything and with no capital?

Nothing, because that is what grows without capital and it grows anywhere. Our chance is here to give Africa what it needs right now, and we are in the business of Transforming Africa with a future clientele of about 3 billion in the next generation that is what they meant when they said *"the future is Pan African"*.

Africa is the next big thing and Zimbabwe should be the window for capital flow for African Transformation because they are going to innovate the African market and capitalize on it. If we are positioned as the pockets of the African mega projects and the program of African transformation, then boom! We are going to create a critical mass that when they come, they attract others and we just become a place where every believer wants to be in (*Heaven*). They are all going to be affiliated with this place, wherever they are Zimbabwe should that home that they never had.

We are going to open up to our African brothers first for we cannot have a party without telling our neighbors, neither can we have a party without inviting our fellow Africans first. We are going to have the best talent working in Zimbabwe from Africa and the world, but I am quite confident that Africa shall be home to plus or minus forty percent of the global youth population.

Consequently, we shall be a center of innovation and value creation too which means that financial partners have a greater role to play in materializing our ideas and we too have a role to play in enabling them to make more money. We are willing to work with whoever wants to work with us basically to exchange value for its all about what you can offer this world and not who you are.

When you become relevant and important you create value that you do not need to introduce yourself and it is the other way round people would love to introduce themselves to you. If we position ourselves to be an AFC (African Financial Center) then we do not need to go around flying for capital but instead capital will come flying to us for Africa will be of global importance by then.

This means our infrastructure will be modernized as per international standards and our vision of becoming a world-class country will in the long run be a reality without straining ourselves. By then our vision will be creating value for us and positioning us for another relevant position in the future.

Our airports will have to add more routes to them and in the long run we tap more taxes from the operators and that's more wealth being increased in our coffers. We will have to build more hotels and resort areas for our guests and that is a blessing in disguise for it will promote our tourism with our places like Victoria Falls, Chinhoyi Caves, Hwange National Park, Mana Pools, Lake Kariba too many to mention.

We can be home to be the best universities in the world because of our global importance and we attract the crème de la crème of the world. In the long run they will be part of our local labor markets providing diversified thinking and ideas in our economy, and through that we shall achieve global competitiveness.

Through creating a financial hub of global importance, it is also a win for our local banks for they will begin to partner more with other foreign partners as intermediaries for example foreign exchange remittances and even major international transactions. They can also start expanding into our regional markets to tap into other banking sectors imagine CBZ in Kampala or Steward Bank in Kigali, Accra or even as far as New York that is how global connectivity could help in increasing our relevance globally. It will also be a gateway for us to serve in the global markets and places we haven't tried and that is more wealth coming in our way.

Another sign that we might not see is that the African Union also aspires to have an African Monetary Institution and even Stock exchange but where do they get it without creating a global presence in trade and commerce? Again do you not see that fate is presenting the opportunity to us but it is not saying directly to us, *that Zimbabwe this is your moment we just have to grab it"*, whether we like it or not this is Africa's moment and because of its huge consumption power it will need an African Stock Exchange (ASE) because Africa is the future market worth trillions of dollars and one day it will need a stock market and what if it gets situated in Zimbabwe?

Will there be any nation that dares to mess with us for we will be having a stronghold of 2.5 to 3 billion people across the continent. This means even big financial giants would begin to bid to be on our Stock Exchange and it is going to be a very prestigious stunt to be listed on the African Stock Exchange.

The future is full of endless possibilities for those with a spirit of adventure and those who will catch up with it when it is young and grow with it. By the way those who solve bigger problems will have bigger rewards for it is just what it is, and I will repeat this whoever solves Zimbabwean problems solves the African problem and shall be rewarded immensely that I know.

We are talking about the capital mystery that remains unsolved ever since Kwame Nkrumah's time. Now imagine the results if we solve it!

Zimbabwe has the tools to transform the situation in Zimbabwe and Africa at large for we have visionaries and quite loads of financial technocrats to create the next biggest financial centers in the world. Steve Jobs is usually accredited by the statement *"The ones who are crazy enough to think that they can change the world are the ones who do"*.

I would love to see those crazy ones who push the human race forward coming from Zimbabwe. Let history remember us as the madmen of yesterday who shaped the present.

The Common Man

"To measure a country's success by GDP is measuring things but not satisfactions"-Julius Mwalimu Nyerere.

Economic development is what we want, and I believe it should not only be measured by what our nominal GDP is, nor what is our purchasing power parity, but by the quality of life of the common man.

We should start looking at how many states of the art schools we have built-in Binga, Mwenezi or Uzumba. We have to look at the state of our medical facilities that do they suit the international standards despite being meant for poor people because they are still people and are shareholders in the Gross Domestic Product.

We should focus on building homes for our people and not just shelters that put a roof over their heads. Common people are human too and they also need facilities like water, electricity and even a bit of space. This is no longer a century whereby people have to go to the well or the nearest 5-kilometer borehole to fetch clean water that should be in the tap and accessible from their homes.

This is not the century to be going around looking for firewood to cook but they should be many energies that are sustainable and renewable like solar or even electricity it is a basic human right that everyone ought to access in the 21st century. This is also the era to be investing a lot in the people we should be focusing more on human development to enhance the capacity of our people in creating their destiny.

We need to update the thinking of our people to that of a higher economic state so that they develop their country. If we update the thinking of our people from the survival mode to that of a middle class and prosperity-driven life, then we can build the *Lion economy of Africa.*

By upgrading the thinking of the people to that of a prosperity state subconsciously you grow the economy for you to increase the needs of the people and then the markets explode.

If people's mindsets are shifted from the old paradigms of living in huts and so long as they have a roof and learn the benefits of having a home equipped with smart televisions, tumble dryers, washing machines, dishwashers and even having cars for easier mobility, imagine how much money would be in circulation from the companies that manufacture and sell these things. Imagine the energy that would have been saved from doing daunting tasks for more innovative work.

The reason why people do not have these things is that they are not developed enough, and they lack the understanding of these things. That is why I am for development more than just growing the economy.

I am more of development to growth for I believe that development adds more value and is effective whilst growth is accumulation is size and numbers. Growth is like giving a monkey one billion dollars when it needs bananas, but the monkey doesn't know what has been presented in front of it. The monkey might go for days hungry without knowing how much it possesses, how many bananas and plantations it can buy and even import the bananas in varieties because it can. But in its eyes, it just sees an accumulation of papers that cannot do anything.

Then in contrast, development gives more capacity and potential to one in reaching their desired state, it is a matter of what you do with what you have and not what you have. Once an individual is developed then they have many options in what they have because of their capacity and they are not limited by the scarcity of resources.

How was Japan able to bounce back after the Second World War, despite being *"A little island with a few natural resources"* and becoming the third-largest economy today by nominal GDP? It is because their people were developed from the war hangover and broadened their horizons from that of scarcity to that of come what we may rise again.

Another Asian Tiger South Korea was so poor, and backward after its founding and the Korean War in the 1950s and around the same period an African state Ghana was founded in 1957. South Korea with barely any natural resources nor financial muscle around that time has risen from Third World to First World and today it is part of the G20 nations. In comparison, Ghana is still a third world nation though its economy was one of the fasted-growing economies in Africa in 2018.

The reason why these two countries are quite different is because of human development the people of South Korea were capacitated to rise above all odds to transform themselves into a nation of global importance. There were also coups and assassinations in South Korea and also in Ghana, but it is more about developing their people with the capacity and potential to transform from the mud to the highest state that made South Korea different.

Every country has got problems and is born with them, and no country is born an economic saint with everything but instead the people need to be capacitated to have an inventive mindset to create new technologies that bring wealth. If you give a local tailor, the mindset to start a clothing line will their lives ever be the same? They will have a growth mindset of going global and then they employ others, creating wealth and changing their lives and also for those around them.

Developing the masses will develop our nation too for the mindset that they have won't be limited to what's there but will forever stretch to having no limitations. People become free thinkers who see no boundaries and are driven more by the prosperity syndrome of wanting to be the best they can be.

Your mind will never stretch to what it has never been exposed to before, and if you are exposed you have unlimited options and that is what the 21st century needs people who can rise above all odds in their thinking despite their limitations.

It was through Henry Ford's vision to have an automobile for the common man that he wanted the common man to be part of the American Dream that saw him becoming one of the most relevant men in American and world history to the extent that he has been identified as the inventor of the car because of the success that he got.

Ford did not only change the industry, but he changed the way people lived and even how businesses were done by perfecting the assembly line and even the way he gained the market share. He grew the middle class of American society by doubling the wages of the *"common men"* from about U$2 to U$5 a day and the common man became part of the American Dream.

If you watch the documentary series called; The Men who Built America, you will realise that Ford did create a new business model for the next generation of American entrepreneurs to build goods for the common man. During Ford's time companies like: Harley Davidson started to create motorcycles for the common man as well, mass production in chocolate factories came too cosmetics were distributed from Hollywood to the common people. Now the market had exploded with goods for the common man, and their spending increased, and prosperity was shared amongst everyone.

Bill Gates had the vision to have the majority of computers using Windows and he too knew that every home should own a computer one day it was also a vision that incorporated the common man, today he is one of the richest men in the world and many people have computers.

Knowing the importance of everyone and the value they can create for you if you advance them is the greatest thing one can ever do in business and leadership also a contributing factor towards developing an economy. The common man is a common market and common resource every business and government ought to serve if they need to advance.

The other thing we forget is that within the common man lie solutions too and they make up the majority of our nation their concerns should not be ignored and forgotten. They have the power and they are the foundation and walls of society they are the ones that give strength to society. If walls are shaken society falls to the ground but thanks to the common man that makes the foundation society can rise again to its might because of them.

Those at the top in business the captains of industry and high-level officials are just the roof of society that is seen from afar and they are anchored by the common man who makes up walls and the foundation of our society. Without walls would a roof exist? No, it will just remain as a roofing material on the ground, I guess. The common man is like the heart of a society that pumps blood and gives life to society.

Our society is a body and nobody can have a life without the heart. The common man gives life to ideas and they work on them to create value and the dream becomes a reality. They are the ones who work hard, day in day out cracking their heads meaning they are also the brains of the society they produce hormones like value creation, creativity and development.

During election time they are the ones who put politicians in office therefore they hold the keys to society's prosperity, and they can change the status quo for they have the power. Despite being the producers of goods and services in society they are also consumers. They are the real custodians of power and they deserve to be treated like masters, of which they never demand to, and they continue to live like slaves for the sake of society.

Do you not think that these men and women are undervalued? I mean, they are the unsung heroes of society who never ask for fame though they are effective. We can remove the powerful from society and society won't shake for they are just light powered by the switch of the common man.

The common man remains treated like a second-class citizen as if they are the ones that crucified Christ or the ones who ate the forbidden fruit. Yes, you might want to argue that is how the world is, it shall never be perfect and uneven, but I take it as inconsiderate and shallow thinking that is born out of an egocentric worldview.

Yes, the good earth is rich but not everyone will be able to get the rich grains of the gold along the way and it does not make them lesser humans nor does it make the rich powerful gods. If we all become entrepreneurs, then who would work for the other? If we all become leaders, then who would follow us apart from our own shadows?

Or we want to go back to Sir Godfrey Huggins' theory during the colonial era in Zimbabwe (back then Rhodesia) of the *"Horse and the rider"*. In short, he said the white minority were the riders and the black majority were the horses. So, is it now a shift, whereby the privileged few are riding over the commoners? Well I think our relationship shouldn't be a horse and rider's relationship but instead a win-win situation. The businessperson brings an idea; I work on materializing it and you pay me decently so that I can also afford what I created or sell.

To those holding public office I give you my vote, in return you give me what I need. You do not block me from questioning your intentions, because I am the one sustaining you and you should respect my rights as well. It is a matter of, *"I have what you need, and you also have what I need so let us exchange value"*.

Let us do away with dehumanizing people because of their vulnerability and desperation. People need to feel motivated through job satisfaction and getting more and enough money to fulfill their needs, wants, niceties and luxury in this life but the sad truth is the people are just paid *"enough"* and then they are drained emotionally, financially and morally.

If corporates become more purposeful in their cause by putting people before profit they wouldn't spend millions of dollars on motivational programs to cheer up the employees then go back to what demotivates the workers the after the retreat which is the, *"You are very lucky to have a job in this economy, do you know how many people are jobless right now"* treatment. I strongly believe that the same capital can be used to advance the lives of the employees a bit so that they become happy. I guess that is why Henry

Ford said that your first customer is your employee. Maybe that is why he went on to increase their wages yes money is not happiness, but it makes things happen and is a tool to live on day in and day out. Also, the common man needs a decent life too.

It is not anyone's fault, it is a system that was there before we came here and now it is our responsibility to change it, but who would we want to change it when we are the ones presently available? Yes, we respect the idea and honor you, but an idea is nothing until it is worked on. Other people work hard to materialize it and they have to be respected for that is their part, without people your idea would have just been wishful thinking.

Therefore, people need to be paid decently to be able to have a comfortable life whether they are janitors or actuarial workers everyone needs a comfortable life, and no one should be denied their right to prosperity due to their social standing.

I believe that the people hold the keys to high positions of power in government and through that we should start by respecting their will and their interests. When you become part of the central government you are a puppet of the people you are there to safeguard the interests of the common man. Their interests aren't that demanding and power threatening instead all they want is the best that life can ever offer them.

They are in pursuit of happiness, prosperity, comfort and peace basically they are not even asking for too much and they are not asking it from the wrong person but from their servants who are there to serve them. Would it be illegal to ask for treatment from my physician? I do not think so for he is my doctor and I have trust in them that they can deliver.

When you get power, it is like the society has entrusted you with their health and wellbeing you are like a doctor we come to for remedies, your responsibility is our wellbeing and it is our right to be prosperous. Now the problem arises when you do not respect the rights of people and see them as your enemies because they demand something and then exert force on the people to silence them.

No court, no law, no constitution can ever take away the will of the people, the will of the people is divine, and it is a natural law that one can never prevent. It is like life and death no man can give life nor deny death for it is a natural order of life. We were born with inalienable rights that cannot be separated from them like the right to life and even the right to prosperity.

If we desire something, it is our birthright and no man can starve us of what we desire; our rights are the water of life and without water creation dies. No one can never take away the rights of people through manipulation and invoking fear, for the people have the power to put you and remove you since they are the custodians of power.

The social contract was designed not to protect the governors from the governed but for the governors to protect the will and the interests of the governed. Knowing that we are all humans and one day we shall all leave this earth should be a constant reminder for those in power to cater for the common man.

No one can be powerful forever, because either way our common denominator will surely one day knock on the door and take us to a land where we are all equal and powerless which is the graveyard. We are all temporary on this earth we just in passing to a land where we all do not know where it is, so why should we live in fear and hatred of another?

I believe that the common man is not your pawn for you to be in power, and their emotions aren't supposed to be used as a chance for politicians to get into power and then ignore them. It is no longer the time to do rhetorical representation assuming that you know what the electorate wants when in fact you do not care and only know what you want.

The common man is not a sacrificial pawn to safeguard the elites' interests, they mean no harm to anyone they just want a secure future like anyone else. We cannot afford to build our political relevance upon the misery of a man who is suffering, do we not have as a conscience? Are we machine men?

Suffer first then vote for me strategies do not work, if we are there to serve the people let us serve them even without a political office. Political office is not power it is just an administrative position that you are entrusted with by society. *"A title does* not make a man but a man makes a title", so if you are waiting for a title to serve us please do not come to us because you have already failed us from the beginning and you too have failed.

Power is the ability to change the existing order and one who changes the situation has got the power and not the one with a title.

Unity and Patriotism

If there is anything that our nation needs now is the spirit of collective effort and oneness in our national affairs. Our politics has become so toxic that it has divided us more than uniting us and things are done on partisan lines and there is always a divide when it comes to doing national things.

Our history has become so much aligned to the liberation movement, and those who do not support it usually end up hating our history and heritage thinking it is a party

164

affair. I think that when a freedom song is sung it should ignite a sense of passion, appreciation and patriotism amongst all citizens for that is where we all came from it is part of us. Look at the USA children as young as eight years old, how proud they are when they sing their Constitutional song *"We the People"*. It is simply because the birth and building of their nation are not credited to one party, neither the Whigs (Republicans) nor the Democrats but to *The People*. So even the present generations are reminded that they too can make their country a better place and history shall reward and remember them.

Even our Southern neighbor South Africa's history never divides them whether it is the ANC, EFF nor any other party there is a time when they are both reminded of what they share the journey they walked together to be where they are today. Yes, ideologies might differ because we cannot all think alike but history is not meant to idolize the liberation movements only but to remind the people that no matter how hard the road is, they have done it before, and they shall prosper. Solomon Mahlangu, Steve Biko, Chris Hani, Robert Sobukwe and even Nelson Mandela are all celebrated as national heroes, but they came from different parties and organizations.

Our emblem our national bird, the Zimbabwean bird can never fly to its desired destination with only one wing neither the right alone nor the left alone. Right now, it seems as if the right feels as it is always right, and no one should dare to mess with them. Then the left does not want to cooperate, or it is always left behind, then the bird never flies it falls back to the ground and wishing that it could fly the other birds of the skies. The bird forgets it can also be like that once it combines all its wings again. Unity and patriotism should be the gospel that our leaders push for as they write a New Testament of Rebuilding Zimbabwe.

When we are divided, we fail to find common ground and we even use that common ground so that we emerge on top of one another. Right now, the common denominator is poverty and economic paralysis that needs healing, yet we are dodging and avoiding one another to create a solution so that we take all the credit back to the party! Instead of giving the victory to the people, when did we lose when we were united? We had colonialists in our land, and we defeated them when ZANU, ZAPU and the masses united to fight the enemy. We had a fallout at one point in time after independence and we united, and peace and tranquility came to our nation. We had the 2008 crisis but what happened after we created a Government of National Unity (GNU)? We didn't go far but we were able to mitigate the crisis that we were facing and even to create a peaceful environment for our country.

I hope you see that with an individualistic approach we can never be prosperous as a country. The ruling party has to engage the opposition and the citizens to find a way if the stakeholders' wishes are not respected then that organization is likely to fall, because it forgets its moral obligation of considering everyone who is affected by its actions.

When a country is divided into partisan lines the not so favored ones will feel alien at home and home in an alien land, their level of patriotism just fades, and their heart is no longer at home and they look at places where their talent and meritocracy is honored and materializes.

It is a natural law that everyone will ask themselves what am I getting out of this? Do I eat patriotism? Many people are driven by the rewards than the purity of the intent which is why they are doing something, so as long as they can build a house in a mountain drive the latest car, earn respect amongst their colleagues and live comfortably then yes, they go for it.

I remember growing up when I wanted something from my mother she would say, *"I will buy it for you if you come first in your class"*, then I would work hard to be come first in my class. Honestly speaking, my mother understood the importance of rewarding the spirit with material and it does not change as people grow, they become more materialistic. Even for most of us from many corners of the world we were told that Santa Claus would bring us presents on Christmas eve if we were good all year and if we were not, we would get a stick, so we always tried to be good all year round. This shows how many people are driven more by the rewards associated with something than the punishments and the purity of intent

Patriotism is not invoked by chanting empty slogans and TV programs that talk about it, yes there is nothing wrong with such information and phrases but people need to see the rewards of it.

If we talk about patriotism and a Zimbabwean citizen comes with an idea to change Zimbabwe, then it is ignored and then the officials listen to a foreigner do you think it is fair on their part?

I know of a girl who always had a dream to work at the Avenues Clinic ever since she was young now, she is training to be a doctor but when she becomes a doctor and gets paid peanuts it doesn't mean she is unpatriotic if she asks for more money on the streets. It means she needs a reward for her childhood dream and enough motivation to wake up and serve her country every day.

I also know of a roommate I had in high school who cried one day when he realized that Zimbabweans do not use airplanes that much and today, he is Australia studying aeronautics to make Zimbabweans fly more often. Again, if he comes to Zimbabwe and his merit is not honored, he will look at the rewards of staying here against how much his parents invested into his education and then he leaves for another country that honors his merit and then grows their already big aviation industry.

These people do love their country and their country has to love them back for if they do not get that reciprocated love back it is quite draining on their side, they go into the world to look for a new love that respects and honors them. We have many Zimbabweans making waves across the world professionally, as entrepreneurs, sportsmen and the list go on. All these people are there because of the rewards.

Do you think if sportsmen were rewarded handsomely here would Chavanga, Mtawarira and Pocock be abroad playing rugby when they were made here in Zimbabwe? If business agreements were honored, would we have lost many of our businessmen staying abroad and investing more in other countries?

How many professionals are all across the world from Zimbabwe? How many citizens have just left this country for peace of mind to do menial jobs in the UK and USA leaving their high-level jobs here?

It is because of the rewards they get after they put one hundred percent compared to the peanuts they get here. If America didn't pay its people enough, I bet they will be all over the world looking for better rewards and the American Dream would be an empty slogan.

They say charity begins at home and does not end there but if a home doesn't love you back then you cannot keep on giving love where all your efforts go astray. If we reward our people with the rights they deserve, honor and pay them more than where they want to be, would they leave this country?

If we want to return a Zimbabwean engineer from the UK, we need to create comfortable and motivational conditions for them to come back here because only a very few people will leave a comfortable life for a hard one in the name of patriotism.

The reason why Napoleon created the Legion of Honor was because he wanted to honor meritocracy in France at the same time fostering a sense of having many great minds, creating the might of his nation and avoiding losing his people to countries like Britain. If we do not honor our great people like the Masiyiwas, Nakambas, Hlongwanes and too many to mention do you think they will stay?

Patriotism is not just something we invoke in our people through slogans but by noticing their might and rewarding everyone accordingly so that they do whatever they do wholeheartedly. I believe that patriotism is a constant reminder and a result of motivation that you are part of the nation because we all need a reason to wake up every day doing something like what Zig Ziglar said that *"Motivation is like bathing hence that is why we recommend it every day"*.

If we return all the students that go to the best institutions in the world, all professionals working for big corporations, business people in other countries and also engage the ones here at home? Don't you all think Zimbabwe will transform itself? But they will come when they feel that something big is in the pipeline for them and they come for the rewards.

Some say, *"home is the starting place of love, hope and dreams"* but is it home when your dreams are murdered, your rights are not respected with every day the future looking bleak and your hope becoming uncertain? So instead people leave in search of another home.

Patriotism without rewards to the people is like, waiting for a boat to take you to Mars it doesn't work maybe it will in the next life after we reincarnate. Our people love this country and they also need to be loved by this country, therefore, let us build a society that rewards, honors, notice the meritocracy and work of the people in return they shall give their all to this nation they love.

That is how we create a patriotic society with people that pledge to serve their country not through words but in their deeds. Through men and women who know that they owe allegiance to their nation we will build a strong, resilient and prosperous modern-day nation. Of course, words have the power to inspire or destroy but in the long run, everyone is moved more with the rewards that materialize if people see the material benefits of being patriotic I tell you we would not even have papers lying around in the streets without anyone picking it up, it will be more of a collective effort towards things than it wasn't me or it is not my job that we have today.

CHAPTER SIX - THE ROAD TO THE FUTURE

We are not going to wake up developed instantly with the click of a button which means there is a time for us to cross the bridge from the point of destitution to the point of prosperity that my learned countrymen would call *The Transitional Period.*

The sad thing is time will be moving and does not stop just because we are crossing the bridge life goes on. Yes, people need hope and motivation but they do not eat it, it does not pay their bills, it does not put money in banks, it does not build and revive industries and won't heal us when they are ill.

Hope instead is a state that is assured by a promising future and no one will see a promising future when they have no money in the bank, but it is reflecting in their account, when they cannot afford basic social services like health or even paid enough to survive.

I know some might want to equate Zimbabwe's story to the *Biblical Exodus of the Israelites* but along the way God would provide the Israelites with what they needed but let us not forget that the Israelites were there by God's plan and we are not coming from slavery.

This is a man-made problem and we do not need to point fingers we know that our levels of corruption, mismanagement and lack of foresight have put us in this mess, so we have to find a way and ask for His humble blessing and forgiveness.

Honestly speaking we have a National disaster; our industries are dead as if they were bombed in the war with the others' days being numbered and they need to be rescued.

Our country is broke than ever before, banks are there, and we have no money, it is available on the parallel markets. Doctors are striking, teachers too and no one is really happy with the situation and everyday prices are skyrocketing.

Such a situation will never give anyone optimism and hope about the future because they are contained by the existing and immediate realities that are quite draining. Many feel that they cannot predict the future and why they should bank on it and become prisoners of hope?

Some feel that they shall remain hanging on the bridge forever and where they are, at the end of the river. It seems as if when they feel that they are getting nearer and nearer, the bridge keeps on getting longer and longer. At first, they thought maybe they had reached the end when they had removed Mugabe from office but no it wasn't the end, now they are back on the draining road again.

Things are getting worse and they just waiting for a signal, but it seems as if it not coming. Therefore, I would love to ask Zimbabwe what is the way forward?

The Strategic Humanitarian Intervention Programme

Below is an architecture of the Strategic Humanitarian Intervention Programme designed by Hannington Mubaiwa.

THE ZIMBABWE STRATEGIC HUMANITARIAN PROGRAM

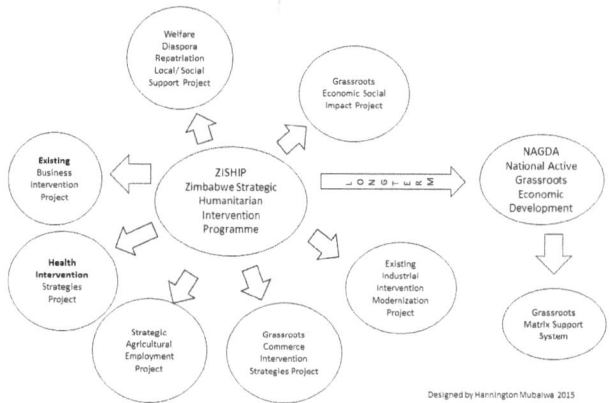

Designed by Hannington Mubaiwa 2015

Many nations have been through worse, even the world giants have been in a sign of destitution with no hope but today they are the envy of the world it's just a phase. The United States of America had The Great Depression in 1929 which had disastrous effects both industrially and socially, but they bounced back and today they are the number one economy.

China was just an isolated country with many peasants but today they are the biggest rival to the United States politically and economically. Japan we all know what happened after Hiroshima and Nagasaki, but they rose and became the second-largest economy for quite a time till they lost the spot to China recently and now stands at number three in the world by nominal GDP (Gross Domestic Product).

You see, we are not the first ones so the world will never lose sleep over that even more countries will pass through that phase. Economies go through such phases of health and sickness like humans so it will never shock people that people get sick because it is natural.

When you fall into the pit make a plan to come out yourself, for your life is in danger other people's. You have to be strategic in exiting that pit because if you are not, you will find yourself back in that pit again. To solve Zimbabwe now the crisis has to be mitigated first before we begin the Transformational process.

It is like preparing the land where we want to build our house, we cannot build our house on land that is full of grass and thorns. We need a program that removes grass for the land that we want to build our house upon. That is where Hannington Mubaiwa's idea of a Strategic Humanitarian Intervention Programme comes into effect to mitigate our problems socially and industrially. It is there for people to hold on to as the nation is being fixed like I said that life goes on, people need food, houses, schools, people get sick and hospitals need to be functioning, our backbone industries need to be working, our banks need money to get things running in our economy, collapsing industries need to be saved and the dead ones need to be revamped before we build new ones.

We need something to get life running as we build a long-lasting and sustainable one. It is just a temporary shelter for the nation as they build their new home that is resilient, prosperous and sustainable. This program aims at not only giving people social welfare, local support services, and industrial intervention but to create a new economic vision for Zimbabwe.

This initiative should not be run according to Partisan lines but on a single national platform which a neutral leader either a business leader, civilian leader, a church leader or anyone who is not a politician. Because this is a plan to mitigate problems that we face socially and industrially hence it requires a more social and industrial approach to a political one. This is a plan to get us going as they get the *"politics of this country right"*.

This has to be a People's adhocracy which special imperative to mitigate our problems faster as we can to save our country from the mud it is in right now. It is like putting an emergency wheel on a vehicle so that it can move to its next destination and then when it gets there, we change the wheel.

What we are doing is getting our vehicle moving as fast as we can so that we finish the journey and get a new one. It is not just about solving problems that should and must be our imperative it is also about growth and real growth is in transformation.

Hence, after we create a taskforce and raise the necessary funds to improve our local services, reviving and revamping industries, redeem our banks, support our backbone industries, create strategic employment vocational training in more technical courses, diaspora Repatriation, and even social welfare.

Why an Independent Taskforce

As young as I am and with my little experience, I know that when you talk about something people usually want to know not mainly what it is or what it does but who will be in charge.

Well, I shall answer you that this program shall be spearheaded independently from the political parties and should be driven on a Non-Partisan front if it means completely different and unknown people let it be so long as they get what it is and can get us out of this mess.

With all due respect we cannot give it to an already busy person or person running another organization for they already have a lot on their plate so we cannot afford to give them some more before they finish what they have I am afraid it will remain an impending project.

No one can be in two places at once, so it is a mission that requires commitment and the drive to see the nation prosper. I believe that if they want to assist, they are kindly welcome as advisors from their expertise, but we have many people who can do it who just need to be given the opportunity to do lead this initiative.

This is a matter of urgency and it requires whoever leading it to be committed so one has to choose between their business empires or to fix the situation.

I feel that this project should be done independently from politics because politics has no sense of urgency the political parties are held more accountable by the party's central committees. This is a matter of rescuing ourselves so anyone with an idea can lead the process so long as it is powerful enough to get us to a safe place.

I think the other issue is about trust no one is going to see the sincerity or the purity of the intent if it is spearheaded by politicians because our politics is toxic and full of negative energy right now.

Even if we give the opposition this as a shadow project it is likely to fail because of the model that their opposition (the ones in power) will try by all means to make it a failure to be politically relevant.

Even if it becomes a ruling party project those who do not support it will just see no relevance in it and say, *"It is just a political move to divert our attention from the existing problems"*.

I hold nothing against no one, but I believe that these projects should be put in the hands of *"Non-Partisan and Non-Aligned Players"* so that people embrace the seriousness and sincerity of such initiatives.

There is a time when a nation needs to adopt a stance of *"Positive Neutrality"* in nation-building and not to choose sides for this is not war. We want people who do not see things in black and white but in high definition in all dimensions, what we want is something tangible and not to care about who brings it.

Hence, if one is to lead the SHIP (Strategic Humanitarian Intervention Programme) they should be a completely different person who is not sucked in the system even if it means them being a Zimbabwean based in the diaspora I do not care so long they know what it is and what to do.

On Solving the Cash Crisis

One of my friends once cracked a joke about Zimbabwe saying that the only two certain things in Zimbabwe right now are death and long queues. Well, we all know that in every good joke there is an element of truth if you read in between the lines.

Look at the situation around you like a person who is coming to Zimbabwe for the first time. Coming from the airport along Airport Road the first thing you likely to see is a long queue of cars for petrol and diesel, fifteen minutes later you are in the Central Business District the next thing is people are in a long queue at a bank. Hang around in town till peak hour when people are going back home go to any bus terminus the next thing is people are in a long queue for the cheap ZUPCO buses and minibuses.

This has become the normal routine for Zimbabweans to have queue after queue to get things like fuel, money, and transport. On the bank scenario your employer pays your monthly salary it reflects in your account then you go to the bank on to realize they have daily allocations and a limited number of people to give. It is usually a race to get there early so that you can get your money.

Sometimes you go there early and there is no money for you instead it is a wasted effort and a draining process for most people. This problem has been there for over four years now and efforts were tried to mitigate the problems, but they did not work out.

The market forces were bigger than the solution itself hence we are where we are today, and the situation has even gotten worse.

Because the Bond Notes were rated at par with the US Dollar people trusted the US dollar more it disappeared on the market and then it was controlled by the parallel market. The parallel markets now determine the rates with prices being charged in US dollars or the equivalent and when in reality people earn in RTGS dollars.

On the electronic money side some companies have seen no point in paying employees through the banks when there is no money in the banks hence, they have resorted to mobile payment systems like Eco Cash.

The problem that now arises is that the Eco Cash agents are imposing their tariffs on top of the already existing ones which they are supposed to be charging people. The madness is that these tariffs differ based on whether you want coins or notes and out of desperation people end up buying their own money to have it.

It never rains but it pours for Zimbabwe because whenever we feel as if we have stumbled upon an answer the market forces are overshadowing them. When you get paid through Eco-Cash you are just given your salary as agreed on your contract and to the employer then they put your money in a mobile bank like the same way they would do in a physical bank.

The forces overpower the whole thing for people to get cash at hand they will need to visit the agents and then they get charged a percentage to get their money out. Even if people get paid through the bank, they need to transfer their money to their Eco Cash to have cash at hand because the banks have no money and again, they have to buy their money from Eco Cash agents. I believe that even if we were to introduce a new currency, we wouldn't be able to mitigate the cash crisis but instead we might worsen it.

The way to go is to find a way from which we acquire a fund through our Humanitarian Programme for Bank Redemption. Our problems are emanating from the fact that our banks are collapsing from the issue of an intangible asset which is *"Trust"*.

Mainly, the fact that the fictitious pegging of the Bond Note at par with the US dollar which saw people trusting the US dollar more and leaving the Bond Notes flooded with no value with people putting their faith in US dollars. This means the US dollar is the currency that is functioning on the ground and the RTGS dollars on paper.

The other thing is people are slowly losing confidence in our banking system and home banking *(under-mattress banking)* is now the norm. There are no deposits in the bank but instead more withdrawals and the banks are left with no money to give to people.

Since the people do not have trust in the measures being implemented to mitigate the crisis and it is more of a panic crisis being caused by a lack of trust in our currency and many have the belief that dollarization (full use of the US Dollar) is the way.

The problem we had from 2015 has not been solved which is banks giving a daily allocation which means we never solved the cash crisis. Therefore, there is need to get our taskforce from the SHIP team (preferably Financial technocrats) to find a model to raise more funds to get our banks running again with adequate money for day to day life of the people.

This is the best way to get the wheels moving again, to get our banks on their feet again for the whole cash crisis thing is adversely affecting a lot of things in our economy. This is just like taking pain killers to mitigate the pain as you seek a long-term treatment hence the Bank Redemption program is to stop the pain that the cash crisis is causing as we cure the sickness to its core.

On Social Services

From a shining beacon of inspiration and hope to African countries our once so-called Jewel of Africa, a shooting star that everyone made a wish whenever they saw it today has become a pariah state.

Zimbabwe has become a global case study of things gone wrong, a case study of how not to do things. The Economic Intelligence Unit ranked our capital Harare amongst the top ten worst cities to live in the world, yes as a patriotic Zimbabwean I was hurt and gutted but the truth is if you take a step back and observe you will see what they mean.

I am afraid that hospitals have become places where the sick go for formality's sake and most hospitals do not have the necessary tools required of healing the ailing, and doctors and nurses have to put one hundred and fifty percent effort.

These medics are now in the streets frequently pleading for increments to live in because looking at the effort they put and the money they are earning it is not a balanced equation the imbalance is negative on their side and yet they put extra effort.

Our hospitals are slowly becoming incapacitated and this is very risky for a nation to have a collapsing health system even if we want to be a prototype nation for African Transformation how can we be one with poor healthcare.

If the people cannot get affordable or even free health care, then our Upper middle-income vision becomes a pipe dream and we should not prioritize anything else before the health of the people.

In rural areas the people there have limited access to healthcare some have to walk as far as ten kilometers to the nearest clinics without medicine or they simply cannot afford.

When it is free healthcare let it not be free of facilities and doctors but just free of charge. Now our doctors all over the country are on strike which means that something has to be done faster with the speed of lightning. On the other hand, our economy is broke, and it has no money but that will not stop people from getting sick and from seeking treatment.

Still on our Social Services apart from the ailing healthcare system we have other problems that need immediate solutions before we embark on the journey of transforming our economy. Our sanitation services are dead and need rehabilitation and to be fixed as soon as possible.

The main concern here is the issue of our water supply, the majority of Zimbabweans do not have access to clean water and what will be the importance of having a strong economy if our people do not have clean water?

The majority of the people in the urban areas especially the high-density suburbs do not have clean trapped water so to mitigate these problems they have dug wells and most of these wells aren't safe as per health regulations. In some parts donors have dug boreholes but the population to borehole ratio is very high hence the problem still resurfaces.

In the medium densities some have tried to mitigate the problem by drilling boreholes, some by installing reserve tanks in their homes where they buy water from those with boreholes. But the thing is not everyone can afford such a *"luxury"* with the current state of our economy.

Besides people cannot go forever living in such a destitute and disastrous state because our economy is broke, these are necessities of life. This is the 21st century and clean water is a basic right, need and people shouldn't need to worry or sacrifice a kidney or a muscle to get water.

Even though, development starts by fixing what is broken so that people can temporarily hold on to something as they build the new. It has become a feature of the day to see young children in the marginalized communities pushing wheelbarrows with water containers, in a long borehole queue whilst their mothers are selling fruits or vegetables trying to fend for the children.

The depth of our crisis has gone beyond what we expected, I believe we all would not want to go on like this and imagine if this is the Zimbabwe in which you would want to raise your children. It is not normal going around with containers of water looking for water to me it is like going around with a container looking for oxygen.

This is unrealistic and with the rate with which we are moving with I do not know what will happen next for it has become so hard to predict what will happen next in Zimbabwe but all I can say an Intervention Plan is an imperative here.

Furthermore, the norm in Zimbabwe is that usually, the children are at the borehole or nearby well looking for water, the mother is at a small market stall vending fruits or vegetables to earn extra income and the father is at a long ZUPCO queue waiting for a cheap bus maybe for the next forty -five minutes or an hour.

Why? Because transport services have become expensive and with the state of things the common people cannot afford. Because of the hikes in fuel prices and basic commodities even our transport fares are increasing and many people are not getting raises as prices shoot up, so instead transport fares alone and they take up about half or a third of their salaries so the best option for now to save themselves is the ZUPCO.

The limiting factor is that the ZUPCO bus supply is lower than the demand and our trains are not working as well so the efforts appear to be in vain to mitigate the transport problems. Our transport services have become so expensive to the extent that cheaper alternatives are lower than the demand sometimes people have to get to work early and they end up sacrificing their little earnings to save their job.

They are paying themselves to get to work so that they can come again because most of their money is used on transportation. Times are tough but people need to move and travel hence the fact that times are tough should not stop people from moving because human beings cannot hibernate and wake up when things are well.

The list goes on and on but the major imperative here is for the task force to raise funds to find a short term and medium-term solution to get the people living normally as we move into rebuilding Zimbabwe. This taskforce should raise the necessary funds to offer solutions within the healthcare system, transport sector and sanitation services.

These are the people that shall be held accountable if anything goes wrong and they are the same people we are entrusting with our livelihoods so they must deliver on what we want them to.

Again, anyone with a plan, strategy and can give people what they need should lead this initiative as well for it is an emergency and we want those who can kick the *Emergency Exit* panel faster to be part of the team.

Protecting and expanding what is already there

Before the modernization process begins, we need to protect the already existing industries and businesses that we already have and save them from collapsing completely.

There is also a need to expand the already existing industries to increase their carrying capacity, to produce and to employ. Our industries are on the brink of collapse and some have already collapsed which has pushed many people into the streets unemployed with the businesses and industries growing broke.

There is no money to drive production and to enhance mechanization too, so our industries are out of date and broke. We are not the first country in the world to bail out its industries and to help the expansion of their industries in dire times.

We can see that the South Korean government did it under Park Hung See when he helped with loans to the existing Korean businesses to create a strong resilient and sufficient Korea. Because of this strategy South Korea expanded its already existing businesses into global giants such as Samsung, LG and Hyundai.

The major reason why I am for Intervention in our already existing businesses and industries is that our people do not have adequate funding to spearhead their projects to be competitive globally.

How can they even buy machinery to meet the huge global demand if they do not have money so, at the end of the day, they are vulnerable to foreign competition and are pushed out of the market?

Just because you are going to get a new pair of shoes it does not mean you do throw the ones you had already, but you add the new ones to your collection. That is the same thing with our income-generating businesses and industries we need to keep them and expand them as we find new sources of income.

If our industries go down, we are going to worsen the situation we all know that more people will be on the streets unemployed and we already have way too many people there. This is a brick by brick approach towards gaining full control of our industrial destiny.

Imagine Samsung started as a company that exported dry fish to China but today it is a global giant that employs more people more than Google and Apple combined. It all started through an Intervention plan by the South Korean government to mitigate the aftermaths of the Korean war and to fast track the transformation of South Korea.

Imagine if we were to do the same in our already existing businesses what would be the impact of the aftermath?

The other thing we should be doing is reviving the industries that are dead and get people to work there. Imagine if we were to revive industries like ZISCO Steel and then expand them what would be the impact on our economy and how many people do we employ?

If we revive what we have and then modernize it, I guarantee you that yes, the road to the future won't be easy but people won't go through extra scorching hell but will see quite a smooth transition from *"The Wilderness to Canaan"*.

Yes, not everyone will have that slice of bread, but it is guaranteed that the majority will have at least something to hold on as they move to the predestined land of honey and milk.

I say, more capital inflow towards funding the revival and expansion of our industries and businesses will not only prevent their vulnerability to the foreign competition but also solve the employment crisis and even might generate some income for our nation in the long run impacting our growth too.

Social Welfare

Lest we forget, the main reason behind this program is to mitigate both the industrial and social impact of our broken economy.

As we all know our crisis has gone beyond being economical alone but to a social one as well. Many people need Humanitarian assistance from food subsidies, transport and even housing subsidies, basically, the social wellbeing of the people should be our major issue of concern.

Whether the economy is performing well or not people need shelter, food and transport to move every day. Therefore, budgets should be allocated and set aside for such welfare programs.

Some people cannot make ends meet and they will need help in their day to day lives for them to meet their basic needs if it means paying them a Living Grant to be able to afford and meet their basic needs we need to do so.

Even if it means opening vocational centers to equip the people with technical skills so that they do not rely on social services forever and that we have more capable people to drive our industries. We also need to fund free education for those who have been affected adversely by the impact caused by our economy.

Bringing Back those desperate in foreign lands

Recently our people have been subjects and victims of Xenophobic attacks in our neighboring economic *Safe Haven* South Africa. Because of the failing economy in Zimbabwe most people have left for better economic prospects and even without a plan and to them they will cross the bridge when they get there.

Now everyone is leaving for better prospects in neighboring South Africa where some get employed, some underemployed and some even not employed.

When Xenophobia comes our people are part of the sacrificial lambs for the rituals and it is slowly becoming a trend in South Africa. The major reason is that to the South Africans we the Foreigners are coming to their dinner table and serving ourselves their food.

Now we need to introduce strategic employment and training programs to bring back those in the diaspora without a plan and give them what to do at the same time equipping them. Our people need to be returned to our country to do something worthwhile at the same time gaining something.

Adopting a Transformational Project

As much as we might want to fix the problems, we have today we must not forget that fixing is only a temporary solution and we need to start creating a new reality for Zimbabwe and in this case meaning we need a Transformational project.

I am quite confident that amongst our people we have Transformational leaders and architects those with the power to dispel old methods by casting a powerful vision and leading idea.

They don't have to be affiliated to the ruling party alone nor be solely opposition members or leaders, professors nor economists but anyone with a powerful idea can do that I believe.

Ideas whose time to manifest has come do not choose the social standing nor power of the man in society to come to life but instead, go to a place where there are motivation and the willingness to drive the idea.

I believe amongst our fellow countrymen there are a few men and women who do not sleep with their heads cracking on what they could do to bring back the pride of our nation.

These are not just citizens at home but also abroad not just the old but the young nor the rich but also the poor, so we never know who holds the keys to the breakthrough of this nation.

My two cents would humbly say that the **Trillion-dollar nominal GDP** vision is not a pipe dream if the right plan is put into place. I believe that a Transformational project vision with a 40-year outlook will get this nation running back on its two legs.

Like I mentioned earlier on in this book most projects fail because of capital constraints and we might say let us do the with the little that we have.

I couldn't agree more but instead will say let us be more ambitious to have a big slice of the Global cake and we can only do so if we have a new financial Map that puts us in a position to compete because we have the resources.

This is our hedge against foreign domination and hegemony because if we try to go slow, we will be eaten already before we walk out of that door because we're so behind.

We need a model that leapfrogs our economy to catch up with the rest of the world, the fact that the 4IR is here and we are three revolutions behind should be a motivational factor serving as a wakeup call when we plan our Transformational project.

Now is not the time to be thinking and going slow it is the time to be doing and faster for the slower shall be outrun and lose the marathon forever sadly.

With the power of technologies what took other countries 50 years should take us half of that because they had no one to ask or learn from so it was trial and error process, they got lost many times till they found their way home.

We cannot afford to get lost when we have the maps in our hands and even advanced features like the GPS, come what may we are getting home as early as we can because we have a path and many tools that can help us get there.

We have to learn from them about the hidden cues and principles and apply them as soon as we can because now is the time to run as fast as we can and keep on running till, we catch up. When others started the race, we didn't hear the sound of the gun so now we have to pay for that.

Another indirect cue for an economic miracle to happen sooner than expected is that our human capital should be developed faster. They need to have the capacity to run their country, the powerful psychological ammunition for stronger mental fortitude and to raise our country to the highest economic state it can ever be.

I believe actions will speak louder than words then we should have an action plan that should empower the people.

I believe that this vision will be powerful enough to give every Zimbabwean the hope and the reason to believe again. The vision must be completely feasible, communicable and clear for most of us.

It should be an idea that we all wake up to and say to ourselves I am going to do this it is part of my generational obligation. The people themselves have to see that this is a feast in which they are invited to the table and they have a steak and stake to also eat on that table.

This idea should be powerful enough that whenever one comes into Zimbabwe whether at Chirundu, Beitbridge, Forbes, at the airport and even in their sleep when they dream of Zimbabwe, they smell that idea floating around and that they are missing out on a lot.

Our New Zimbabwe vision once materialized must be able to attract more resources to grow like how a business offering IPOs but this time with the people coming to it offering it their value.

The new imperative is not to run Zimbabwe like a tuck shop or a market stall but as a business, turning our nation into a Mega Business like what Hannington Mubaiwa suggests! Yes, read that again Zimbabwe is to be run like a huge conglomerate with diversified interests. The people being the shareholders will be getting their dividends whether they are declared or not.

It is because they all hold preferred stocks and they can hold the Board of Directors (**Central Government**) accountable for any mismanagement and anything that ignores the needs of the shareholders.

The role of the government shall be mainly the wellbeing of society, the creation of societal wealth and distribution in a more equitable manner. The government should take our tax money as bonds that we give them, and we require them to pay back to us every day with interest through our social services and our welfare as people.

The other thing is the scalability of the new Zimbabwe vision is not to be solely based on Zimbabwe but to increase it into tapping into the Pan African marketplace. Like I said earlier in this book that we should position ourselves as the brightest star of Africa and be a window for African transformation from the Southern and Central regions of Africa.

We are starting on virgin paper and nothing can stop us from giving birth to as strong giant African baby? We are a virgin nation when it comes to transformation and not an infertile nation. We can create a disruptive revolution that can change the direction of where the world thought it was going to a new one. That is if we see beyond Zimbabwe and begin to leverage the future *2.5 -3 billion population* of Africa.

This project should be a prototype for African nations to embark on sustainable socio-economic transformation and Zimbabwe should be the place where it starts. If it becomes a success in Zimbabwe, then it will encourage other fellow nations to follow suit.

The scope of our vision is not just to rebuild Zimbabwe but Africa as a whole. So, as I said previously that the vision is to look at the future two and a half billion-consumption power of Africa and take is our responsibility to provide for their day to day needs and wants.

Our new imperative should account for Macroeconomic unity amongst the Africans and fostering a spirit of Industrial unity. It must account for the building of a Zimbabwe and Africa that is an economic powerhouse amongst the Big Five economies of the world.

The African lions have to roar for them to retain an important position in the global jungle and Zimbabwe has got a greater role to play in this process. Fate is moving towards our favor, but the thing is we have faced it for too long blindfolded by fear and doubt.

If we try looking at it in a more favorable way, we can all see that we have been given many cues and clues to be great, but we ignore them, now is the time to start moving so that we meet our fate halfway.

Some will doubt, criticize and say it is shall never happen we are just thinking wistfully I do not care and do not care that I do not care because it is not our duty to seek approval from them. Neither do I care if they want or not because a revolution begins with a very few people and ends up spreading like wildfire to many people.

Apple did not start with many people using it, but it was an ambition born in a garage in San Francisco that was going to impact the world later. Dr. Strive Masiyiwa did not start by seeking approval from people but he did so by starting with the end in mind and then walked towards it till he got it.

We might be laughed at or criticized but I tell you that the fate of our nation is not defined or enabled by consensus or by the high approval rating of critics but instead by an accurate architecture of the future. Like what Abraham Lincoln said that *"The best way of predicting a future is by creating it"*. s

It is the scalability of our project and the scope of our vision that will pitch itself to the investors who shall invest capital and even human resources into that project. Here, the odds are that Zimbabwe is going to be a resilient and strong nation we have predicted this bright future for we have already created the future that we want. We have started with a finished product already, so we are now just manufacturing it to come to life.

The other thing is we need to get our ethics in check we cannot keep on running our country in a lawlessness fashion and manner which has resulted in unethical behavior unaccounted for.

No matter how powerful a vision is if it lacks value systems it is like giving an inexperienced ten-year-old an airplane to fly across the Atlantic Ocean with passengers on board.

That is when people begin to apply whatever means necessary just to win, imagine how Hitler ended up being despite having the zeal to change and transform German and restore its past glory.

We do not want our industrialists to use the excuse that just because we need to catch up with the rest of the world, they have to exploit people and overwork them so that they underpay them because they are desperate and have nowhere to go.

Whatever our vision and how far we are beyond we need to have a spirit of Ubuntu and Godliness to care for the next person to consider the future repercussions of whatever we do. Like how a business operates we should always know the impact of whatever we do to our stakeholders (the general populace at large).

In the long run we should also implement environmental-friendly strategies in our industrial projects to protect our environment for already the world has seen enough carbon emissions and climate change is a major issue of concern these days. Because of climate change, in the future water might be a scarce resource in many parts of the world therefore we need to consider that and prevent such a crisis from happening.

It is not just about being a powerhouse now but an issue of sustainability we should not forget that they shall be people coming after us. Talking about the ones coming after us we should not forget that even corruption will not sustain us long enough or cheating will not give us any sustainability but instead short-term gains and sooner or later people will discover it.

Even if they are positive signals and signs, they might be cut short and the miracle might appear to be a myth.

With all that we have been through as a country, we cannot afford to go back to the suffering desert just because of poor ethics. Imagine where German was after the First World War, how they had begun to prosper and how Hitler sent them back to the valley when they were about to reach the mountaintop because of his hate against the Jews and his invasion of Poland.

If we do not work on our ethics, we will go back to *"Egypt the land of suffering"* for life is not run on lies but it is centered on principles therefore we can manipulate the economic statistics, the media but the results will always show. Like what ancient wisdom says that you can never hide three things which are *the sun, the moon and the truth.*

A strong foundation of a nation is built by facing uncomfortable truths and not by singing praises all the time. If we are going to position ourselves as a strong nation, we need to be honest with one another a firm foundation is not shaken by the truths that confront it but instead it is made a resilient one.

Our leaders shall be held accountable by the people they must not get away with everything because they have the power to control the structures. If they do any deals that do not favor us the inhabitants of the land, they should be held accountable because we are heirs of the gains of this nation so our birthright cannot be sold to outsiders whilst we sit and sing praises.

We cannot continue to embezzle billions of dollars and keep quiet when we should be reinvesting that money somewhere or even distributing it amongst our people. Our moral fiber needs recoiling for it won't get us anywhere soon but instead keep us where we are and continue blaming someone for our misfortunes.

If it means that someone has to go to court for throwing a banana skin on the road and be held accountable for it if it means that someone gets fined for Jaywalking and crossing at an uncontrolled traffic area, we have to do that.

Because ethics do not only need to be in government officials alone but in every citizen, people have to feel insecure when breaking the law not to feel abnormal when they spend a day without breaking the law.

Business contracts should be unchangeable and unforgettable hence they should not just be nullified overnight or the "government "should not just take away people's properties just because they have the power to.

Private property should also be protected and respected. Businesses that come to invest in our country should also be of value to our citizens and not to *take all leave nothing,* leaving us with a degraded and a health-hazardous environment.

Let us not forget that even some multi-billion corporations in the world fell not necessarily because their vision was poor but because they had no ethical leadership a basic example is the former Houston based firm by the name of Enron.

When these giants fall the CEOs go home with huge packages but those who workday in day out just go home empty-handed and with an experience that might even be haunting.

Be warned of such huge downfalls that will adversely affect the common man and the future generations. As I emphasized before that we should have visions that are long-sighted, I believe that having ethics and discipline are part of being futuristic.

It pushes you to look for a way that makes both sustainability and profitability co-exist. Therefore, our vision should clarify more on the issue of values systems and reward those who comply handsomely and those who do not should be punished heavily.

One of the reasons why ambitious African projects are not coming to life is that they lack the adequate funding to support it and with no funding you will never finish any ambitious project. Even in the business world, startups would need an infusion of cash to move into scale-ups and if not, they fail to get off the ground.

In national transformation we need to be well-fed with capital for it is the heart that keeps the blood pumping in an enterprise. We can adopt a new financial model apart from the already existing ones that allow us to get more funds to get Zimbabwe running again for example the one from the *Rapid Africa Plan: The Fast Track Modernization of Africa* designed by Hannington Mubaiwa and prototype it in Zimbabwe.

The magnitude of the task that needs to be done should be a pitch on itself to the would-be and potential partners as I said before we should be magnetic enough. If they are blessed enough to see that a revolution is about to come from what we are embarking on, they will invest in the future with us for no one wants to be left out in a historical moment that they foresee is about to happen.

I believe that this project will be innovative enough to attract resources particularly capital because there are trillions of dollars with nowhere to go and they can introduce themselves to us without us flying over to them.

The real deal here is to put money in the hands of the Zimbabwean industrialists and businesspeople who are already in business to grow our startups into scale-ups.

If we want to manufacture cars look for a Zimbabwean already in that field with a proven track record and give them the adequate capital to grow their businesses. This is how we can grow our people and our nation by empowering them that is what empowerment is to me to give one the adequate resources to move to the next desired place.

We are not saying foreigners cannot be business partners, but the deals should also benefit the Zimbabwean people and they should all get an equal share as per their agreed contracts.

What matters here is the issue of capital that we need to create a new model that enables financial access, independence amongst our people so that we have control in our industries and markets protecting us from vulnerability to foreign competitors and hegemony in the name of *Globalization.*

We still have a desire to grow and we need to grow so we can't just give ourselves in because we are weak financially. Our market is vulnerable and is prey which is defenseless and vulnerable to be dominated by foreign competitors because we have no access to a massive infusion of capital.

Just because we do not have claws when we are attacked, we cannot defend ourselves and we become prey. This is what is happening now we are defenseless and when the offense attacks, we are eaten for lunch because we have no cash to keep on financing ourselves to keep ourselves in the game.

I believe that whoever can create a plan with finding a way to provide adequate capital to finance our project then that person, group, organization, consultancy or whoever that is the best strategic visionary partner for transforming Zimbabwe.

The capital question needs an answer and again whoever finds the answer not only solves Zimbabwe but Mama Africa as well. For it has kept Africa stagnant even in nations that are corrupt-free and with good governance and low corruption.

By the way like what I said earlier on if we figure out a way to solve the financial issue Zimbabwe can be a Financial Regional Center in Africa and that will not only give us financial muscle but also give Africa financial freedom in the long run.

I believe we already have the people (laymen) with answers to these problems but they are not just given a chance because their LinkedIn profile is not strong enough, they haven't done it before, so they don't have *"strong credentials"*.

Why do we not try those people for I believe we never know what they are capable of until we give them a chance, first by meeting them and lastly by listening to them and seeing the results. I believe that credentials do not deliver, and you do not need credentials to see and design the future.

Like what Henry Ford once said that he got his answers from the universe to build Ford is what I can tell you that Zimbabwe has everything it needs and the answers to its prosperity are already there within its people maybe the unlikely people.

I am not a prophet nor a fortune teller, but I have faith that our breakthrough or the Transformational project was already designed or it's being designed by someone as we speak but they are not just listened to.

They are afraid that their LinkedIn profile and school credentials are not so strong yet they have a revolutionary idea in them, but they are scared to come out. What they have is what we need right now qualified people by levels of understanding and not labels of knowledge.

In short, the one who knows what to do right now is the one to be in charge of the transformational project and the process. If the turnaround of our economy is going to be an economic miracle, then the process too shall be miraculous and the people who shall lead it to will be new faces not the anticipated ones.

That is why it is called a miracle the unlikely things happen and with unlikely people behind them with unimaginable results.

CHAPTER SEVEN-THE EIGHTH WONDER OF THE WORLD

I still dream the same dream, day in day out I dream of a shining red star that shines brighter from Outer Space and everyone makes a wish whenever they see that star. I see one of the tallest skyscrapers in the entire world in a new city that outshines the megacities of the world like New York, Dubai, Tokyo, London and Shanghai.

I read the papers every morning and they say that is where things are happening, and the economic miracle of this nation had surprised the world for it was just a generation ago to them when that nation seemed hopeless but today everyone is talking about it. The nation has entirely become an *8th Wonder of the World* and many are still in shock that how could this ever happen.

One of the World's biggest Regional Financial Centers is there, and the biggest banks of the world are located there competing with her domestic banks also that have grown to be global brands. She has truly become a place open to her fellow Africans and to the world where things are happening.

All across the world in the best institutions she is a case study of how things are done and the Globe sings praise to what she has been able to achieve within a short space of time.

The world flies in the airplanes made in Zimbabwe across all seas and oceans, now they drive in cars made in Zimbabwe in the streets of New York, London, Tokyo, Mumbai, Sydney and even in Lagos.

The world has woken up and realized that the fourth Industrial Revolution is here and now people are even going to Space for a holiday in space shuttles made in Zimbabwe. The experts say we never predicted this, and her citizens respond calmly that *"you can't predict a miracle"*.

In the streets of Zimbabwe new buildings are being erected every day and the cities are growing tremendously at par with the growing population.

People fly all over from the world to come for our state-of-the-art medical facilities which are affordable and magnificent. The best institutions in the world are coming from and into this land which has become an education destination for international students and a place to be.

The innovation hubs, research, and development centers are now rivals, to the world's best like Silicon Valley, Tsinghua, Munich and to name a few. Now the once so-called remotest areas, the once-forgotten corners of Zimbabwe are destination places for international students with state-of-the-art educational facilities.

These once despised places which used to be areas avoided by people are now part of the to visit list for everyone. I see a new nation being born in Central Africa reviving the might of the Munhumutapa Empire, a nation that roars of greatness and a nation that shall be renamed Great Zimbabwe because of its might and Global competitiveness.

It shall be known as the Lion of Africa and shall roar amongst other big cats of this world like the Tiger economies of Asia. I see the fastest technologies, the next geniuses of this world the next Einstein's and inventors down in Africa and us playing a role in building Africa.

I feel like I have climbed the highest mountain and far away I see a city that is on top of a mountain higher than the one I am on and I see a city on top of it. I see the tallest building in the world with the shape of a Zimbabwean Bird and I was told that it is the new government complex where decisions are made.

Olympics are coming to Africa and Great Zimbabwe has won the bid, new sports, and recreational facilities are being built to prepare us to host the world and welcome them to dream with us the Zimbabwean dream.

New hotels and chill-out places are being constructed, car racing is no longer just in Budapest, Buenos Aires, Tokyo or Dubai but down here and we are there.

People are no longer talking about La Liga, English Premier League, Bundesliga and Serie A. They now talk about our Premier Soccer League and so are people from across the world glued on their seats watching the stars made in Africa.

We can now afford to have the stars of the world come down here and play sports and pay them adequately because we simply can.

Before or after UEFA, the world also waits to watch the CAF has now become of global importance and UEFA's final. Our traditional dances like Muchongoyo, Jerusalem and Jiti are now being taught at dance theatres in our country and across the world like how we used to pay for Ballet and Salsa lessons.

Now even in pop culture our country has been labeled as one of the best countries in the world, the movies now show Great Zimbabwe as a playground for the prosperous and a destination to be. Now the second-hand apparel business is no longer flourishing in the boutiques instead we have departmental stores that are full of designer clothes both local and international.

The lifestyle is no longer survival driven but success-driven with the middle-class growing and the standards changing. Every family has the basics like a car, washing machine, dishwasher, electricity, water access and even high-speed internet connectivity in their homes.

Even in the villages the thinking has shifted people now stay in homes and not huts, the village is just a place where people go for retirement, quiet living and farming but not anymore shall we find the subsistence living.

Banks are there, malls, recreational facilities even state of the art hospitals and access to clean water and technologies.

The atmosphere is just that of success and a magnificent living no matter where you go you can breathe it like you can breathe the smell of teargas in a protest. The quality of life of the lowest citizen is ten times more than what used to be the life of the average citizen just a generation ago.

A child from Binga now has the dream of changing the world, they too dream of bringing the world into Zimbabwe. They dream of becoming the next astronaut, the next real estate mogul in Space their vision and thinking is just a million times more than it was a generation ago.

The thinking is just entrepreneurial and just about adding more value even a person who owns a small tomato garden is thinking about how they could add more value to their tomatoes.

The airports are getting busier day by day with people traveling across the country and the world. An airplane is no longer a luxury to the masses but instead a faster way of getting where they want to be.

Everyone has got even holiday accounts to travel during holidays and it is not just for the elite but instead, for everyone people now understand the importance of traveling.

Now people are obsessed with traveling to the extent that in the country we now have spaceships like air buses carrying people to and from the earth to the Moon and Mars. The people of Great Zimbabwe are part of the people on the Globe that enjoy the highest standards of living in the world not just because they have become a trillion-dollar economy. Instead it is because the nation is now more of a welfare state with the Central government understanding that their role is to uplift the standards of people.

No one is homeless the government has engaged in public housing projects and therefore no one sleeps on the streets at night unless they are on night patrol or something like that.

No physically challenged people i.e. (the blind, deaf, mute or handicapped) are on the streets selling airtime or begging but instead, their welfare is being taken care of by the government and if they want to work, they can and they are also special placements for them in every company.

The unemployed are also taken care of and given grants by the government and the government agencies are helping them look for jobs that best suit them whilst they earn a living sum of money every month.

Our public hospitals and clinics are free, and everyone is getting access to healthcare for free which is not free of doctors and facilities but only free of charge.

When our local doctors fail to find a remedy for you, the government hires foreign experts or send you abroad for that treatment on the government's tab. Public education is free from pre-school to tertiary institutions and you can learn as much as you want now because your citizenship alone will pay for you.

If the courses that you want are not available here, you are sent abroad and on the condition that you come back and use your newly acquired knowledge to benefit the Zimbabweans because your schooling was paid for by every Zimbabwean.

Who knew that one- day people from the teapot-shaped Zimbabwe would be living in such luxury and comfort and amongst the prosperous nations of the world?

Zimbabwe has not only changed the way the world sees it but instead it has changed the world in the way it eats, drinks, walks, dresses and even fly. Our foods are now being sold at competitive prices with other countries people now buy mutakura amongst foods like Sushi.

At gatherings people across the world want cooks who can make Zimbo the same as a cook who can make Thai or Japanese it is just how Zimbabwe has made a footprint that is traceable on the global arena.

Our drinks from soft, traditional and even alcoholic are now part of the big boys' club and the taste of it just brings people down here in Africa in our great nation of Zimbabwe.

Our shoes and clothes are there all over the world and our brands are counted on they no longer mention Armani without mentioning our local brands. They won't mention Nike without mentioning our sportswear too.

In the skies they are flying all across the world in Zimbabwean planes, jets and helicopters. Now the world not only dreams of the Zimbabwean dream but eats, breathes, drinks, wears and walks it. Zimbabwe is now a part of them, and they are part of it too, I guess.

For every construction vehicle in the world that is available about forty percent of them are at work in Zimbabwe and almost every day a modern building is being erected whether it's a business tower, housing project, school, hospital or even shopping mall every day we are witnessing something new.

New hotels, new office spaces to let are being built, the back of the building entrepreneurs are moving into the new office spaces.

Zimbabwe is transforming at a pace never seen before and every meeting you go into three out of five meetings it's a pitch for a new business venture that might change the world. I guess the Masiyiwas', the Mataranyikas, the Ncube's and the Maweres created a path and invoked a spirit of endless possibilities and the new generation of entrepreneurs are following suit.

On public transport it is very rare to hear people whining about the state of the nation but instead people are having conversations about prosperity and business. Things are happening in Zimbabwe and even the world headlines and tabloids say so and no one can deny that fact.

The most ambitious projects the world has ever seen are taking place here in Zimbabwe we no longer talk about the Burj Khalifa as the tallest we are talking about a new one in Zimbabwe that the world has never seen and the closest they saw it was in a 2018 movie called Skyscraper.

The question of the day is why are they doing it? The answer is the sleeping lion of Africa has finally woken up and the world can even hear it roar in its silence.

No one ever saw this coming but today we are here in the land of honey and milk our predestined land, our promised land. Now we sit and reminisce of how we got here and even the world testifies with us but we both fail to explain how it even happened to us.

It's just a wonder! To many, they are still in shock and think maybe it is just dream and maybe they will wake up one day and find themselves in long fuel queues, or an economic crisis but days pass by and the blue sky is turning grey with no calamity of such sort befalling on the people.

"To the young and not so old; let me tell you the red star shines bright on the top of the hill and can be seen from outer space, to those with the belief, hope, passion to change the world, the world is yours take all and leave nothing. Every day go to bed with a dream, wake up with a purpose but above all when you see that shining red star that waves on the flag remember that it is more powerful than the shooting star hence, I urge you to make a wish and believe it for together as a nation we shall achieve whatever that you wish."

In my eyes I can see the promised land, I can see what it looks like. In my ears I can hear the sound of the train coming to take us to the land and I have no fear for I know soon and very soon we shall be there. Even in my dreams I dream of a land not so far away with people not different from us living in prosperity and truly the envy of the world.

My dear brothers and sisters like what Eleanor Roosevelt once said *"The future belongs to those who believe in the beauty of their dreams"* hence, welcome to the Future.

WHY I WROTE THIS BOOK

Have you ever thought that if you are fourteen today thirty years from now you will be forty- four years old and that is in the next generation? I am twenty years old and in the next generation, I will be fifty a middle-aged man.

There is nothing wrong with growing but growing with accumulating anything that is my problem. You see from my thinking and observation our system is just rotten to its core, our nation has been destroyed to its foundation and it needs to be rebuilt.

If we continue with such a dead system thirty years from now, I will be a struggling middle-aged man probably still under my mother's roof with my counterparts having degrees that they will never use.

I believe that the whole African machine needs a new engine which is transformational change. Apart from being a Pan Africanist also believing that charity begins at home I have the belief that whoever solves the Zimbabwean issue also solves the African problem.

For Zimbabwe to prosper it has to leverage regional integration and to foster African macro-economic unity.

Whilst other nations are planning to have the children who are born today to be able to choose the Moon as one of their holiday destinations when they get to eighteen what are we planning for those born today?

You see we are completely visionless and without vision the people will perish it is not just biblical wisdom but universal truth that a bus with no destination will never get anywhere because it is going nowhere.

We seem to be planning for the next general election and not generation we seem not to see beyond today and the general election. I am gutted by the feeling that we do not have a national vision that goes for the next forty to sixty years and the fact that we wake up to anything and do whatever we can do survive.

I also find it absurd for a 21st century nation to survive without power, water and even diesel and petrol. It's very painful for me that we have to sacrifice a lung to get basic things like water, electricity, petrol and even to buy bread.

I also think that we need a short-term solution to mitigate the problems that we face today so that we get basic stuff without struggling and to get the bus moving so we can get to the next stop and there we will board a new one.

Above all we need a long-term solution which is a new overall vision for our nation that shall position us in our predestined place of being the leading economy in Africa and leading African transformation.

Again as I said earlier on and before that fate is moving in our favor right now Africans want macro-economic unity and we can see it from the just recently signed AfCFTA (African Continental Free Trade Area) but as of now, they are still looking for a way on what exactly to do to make it effective.

Besides the signing of the AfCFTA there is the future 2.5 billion consumption power of Africa that is closer to home basically our new economic plan has to leverage continental integration.

All these are signals that we are ignoring that could drive us out of destitution into prosperity. My wish is that we appreciate what we have before time makes us appreciate what we had, for the opportunity lies within the time of the opportunity and time waits for no man.

Ideas move from places of lower motivation to places of higher motivation.

If we do not see it and seize it then someone might see it and seize it, then we go obsolete. Therefore, I believe that this a moment that fate has created for us and if we seize it with wisdom, history shall remember us and those who come after us shall honor us.

Ultimately, I am inspired by the book of Habakkuk Chapter 2 verse 2 which says that *"And the Lord answered me, and said, Write the vision, and make it plain upon tables, that he may run that readeth it."*

I too have a vision for my beloved nation whom I owe existence to and therefore I have written my vision for my country and made it plain no matter how big it appears nor how small I look that does not matter for I have spoken what I want into existence and the Good Lord has heard me.

The task that lies ahead of us might appear great, but greater is He who is in us than the world and now we humbly ask for His great blessings in rebuilding our nation and restoring what has been broken.

If God created heaven and earth in seven days, then he will move us out of the mud faster than maybe we even thought for He works in miraculous ways.

Believe me, this country shall be the 21st-century miracle, it shall be the reason why the blind want to see, the deaf want to hear and even the mute would want to speak and testify for the Good Lord is on our side and He says ask and you shall be given now we have asked what is left for us is to start moving towards our blessing.

Let us not give up for we are getting there, we have already gone through hell so why should we stop in hell? Always remember that those who climb the highest mountains will always see the best views.

The youth of Zimbabwe you are the leaders of tomorrow and tomorrow is today so whenever you feel like giving up always remember these words that Lee Kuan Yew told the youth of Singapore many years ago on their path to transformation:

"For the young, let me tell you the sky has turned brighter. There is a glorious rainbow that beckons those with a spirit of adventure. And there are rich findings at the end of the rainbow. To the young and to the not-so-old, I say, look at that horizon, follow that rainbow, go ride it."

God bless Zimbabwe infinity times till the blessed call it blessed. Amen!!

Yours faithfully

The Author.

ACKNOWLEDGEMENTS

This book would have not been possible if it weren't of the people who pushed me whenever I felt I couldn't do it anymore and the few people who said yes to me when the world said no to me.

First and foremost, I would like to thank my mother who believes in me more than I do in myself. If it weren't because of my mother's love, sacrifice and prayers I wouldn't be where I am today. I would also want to thank my grandmother for her love, teachings and also raising me to be who I am today. I would also love to thank my other mother, my aunt for hosting me when I was in the final phase of this book and above all her encouragement when I was burnt out. I would also want to thank my uncles for their support in this project it really means a lot to me. Thanks to my little sister Violet for the noodles, teatime and typing the introduction when I had migraines, I appreciate the support. To my entire family thank you for being there for me through the thick and thin.

I would also love to thank the man who dedicated his time, resources, energy and was patient with me for eighteen months that man is none other Mr. Hannington Mubaiwa. Thank you for all the support that you have given me and continue giving me in all spheres of life, I might not be able to pay you back but deep down I appreciate. It is an honor to have coached by you and to be a pioneer student at the Transformational Institute of Human Emergence. It is through the concepts and principles I learnt from you that the foundation of this book lye upon.

Allow me to thank my friend Forget Maporisi, for his moral support and inspiration that he gave me from the beginning to the end. To the long walks, conversations, and constantly checking up on me, I am grateful for the support my dear friend. I would love to extend my gratitude to the Sithole family for hosting me, it is was their house that I typed my first word in this book only God knows how grateful I am. I would love to thank George Zharare, for making time on his busy schedule to read and review this book, for that I am grateful.

I would also love to thank you, for taking your time to read this book you give me a reason to wake up every day in pursuit of the African Dream. For that simple yes, thank you may God bless the works of your hands and the fruits of your labor.

www.ingramcontent.com/pod-product-compliance
Lightning Source LLC
Chambersburg PA
CBHW052127270326
41930CB00012B/2791